T0323950

Holistic Leadership Resilience

Drawing on decades of experience in the charity sector and enriched by real-life examples, this book helps readers to consider how to be a more resilient leader and explores why a whole-life approach could be a gamechanger in today's world.

The world we live and work in has changed exponentially over the last few years, and all sectors share an increased emphasis on sustainability, self-care, and resilience. But these last two concepts appear contradictory: how can we keep bouncing back from setbacks when we need a break? Based on her doctoral study carried out over three years – and almost 20 years heading up the Third-Sector leadership body in Scotland – Patricia Armstrong shows that resilience is much more holistic than previously thought. It's not just about what we do that keeps us resilient; it's also how we think and how we take into account the environment around us. Readers will find new thinking, tools to help assess where focus is needed, and ways to consider proactive resilience through a new lens so that when the next setback hits, the drop is not so deep and recovery is not so steep. This book comes from the perspective of charity leadership and working in the small country of Scotland, but it offers big lessons which are relevant globally.

Current and aspiring leaders working in all sectors will enjoy and appreciate this book's focus on proactive resilience – putting us all in a better position to look after our well-being and get through to fight another day (and maybe even enjoy the challenge)!

Dr Patricia Armstrong OBE has expertise in leadership, governance, and resilience. She led the leadership body for Third-Sector CEOs in Scotland and recently completed her doctorate exploring leadership resilience. Pat also served on the board of the charity regulator. She has a focus on leadership learning across geographies, across sectors, and across disciplines. Her study into a whole-life approach to leadership resilience brings new insights for today's leaders.

Holistic Leadership Resilience

Whole Life Lessons From The Third Sector

Dr Patricia Armstrong

Routledge
Taylor & Francis Group

NEW YORK AND LONDON

Designed cover image: Getty

First published 2025
by Routledge
605 Third Avenue, New York, NY 10158

and by Routledge
4 Park Square, Milton Park, Abingdon, Oxon, OX14 4RN

Routledge is an imprint of the Taylor & Francis Group, an informa business

© 2025 Dr Patricia Armstrong

ISBN: 9781032627182 (hbk)
ISBN: 9781032627151 (pbk)
ISBN: 9781032627212 (ebk)

DOI: 10.4324/9781032627212

Typeset in Sabon
by codeMantra

Contents

Acknowledgements

So many people have supported me through both my research journey and in writing this book. Although there are too many to list here, I hope you know how much you have encouraged, cajoled, and inspired me along the way – I am eternally grateful!

Thank you to my ever-supportive family, who are always there for me, no matter how surprised they are by whatever challenge I decide to embark upon next. Your patience, support, and understanding have been hugely appreciated.

To my early readers, thank you for your belief in me and for sharing your time and your wisdom.

Leaders from across the Third Sector have been my inspiration. I have seen such amazing leadership during some truly challenging times, and I will always be in awe of your individual and collective endeavours to make a difference in this world.

Finally, to all those who participated in my research, those who worked alongside me, and those who supported me and trusted in me to undertake research on top of the day job, I give my heartfelt thanks.

I hope this book will help develop a better understanding of whole-life (or holistic) leadership resilience from the Third Sector – and help share the learning across all sectors.

Part 1

The Research

Chapter 1

Introduction – We Make Plans, and the Gods Laugh....

Introduction

In current times, resilience can be considered by some as a flawed concept. With the focus often on well-being and looking after ourselves, the fact that we should have to keep bouncing back after setbacks – the definition of resilience – even when we need a break can seem contrary to this thinking. But... life often throws us unexpected challenges, and it is important, as leaders and as individuals, to know how to get through the tough times. This book will throw new light on what keeps us bouncing back. It will draw from a 35-year career in the charity sector, for almost 20 years (as CEO of ACOSVO, The Association of Chief Officers of Scottish Voluntary Organisations), when I was working with some of our most inspiring leaders who make a real difference in this world. It is tested and validated through a doctoral research study. The findings show that resilience is much more holistic than previously thought. All areas of life play into how resilient we feel – maybe not surprising in today's "always on" world. It's not just about what we do that keeps us resilient; it's also how we think and how we consider the environment around us.

I will take you on a journey through my own learning, give insights into how to improve resilience in all areas of life, and will include some of my own experiences as well as examples from leaders I've worked with through the years. Hopefully you will find some new thinking, some ideas to help explore where focus is needed, and find ways to consider proactive resilience through a new lens – so that when the next setback hits, the drop is not so deep and the recovery is not so steep. The book may also be useful for those of you who are thinking of embarking on your own academic journey. The path from being an experienced leader to having to look through a whole new academic lens at your topic is both exciting and daunting in equal measures.

My aim is to help you consider how to be a more resilient leader and to explore why a whole-life approach could be a gamechanger in today's

DOI: 10.4324/9781032627212-2

world. We might never quite get to a Zen-like response to crisis, but if we focus on proactive resilience, we'll be in a better position to look after our well-being and get through tough times to fight another day (and maybe even enjoy the challenge)!

There is also the consideration that as we all work towards a more just world, there is much we can learn from leading in the charity sector. What impact does it have when our roles are to make a difference in people's lives and in the world that we live in? All sectors have changed the way they operate, and the world we live and work in has changed exponentially over the last few years. This book will explore how we live and work holistically, how we can stay resilient to make a difference, and how passion for what we do (no matter what sector we work in) can keep us going when things get tough.

This book is split into two parts:

Part one will take you with me on the journey through my research, exploring the findings and then going into more detail on the behaviours, mindsets, and factors I uncovered.
Part two will consider the way forward and what this means for leaders. It will start by looking at the changing world we are leading in, consider some new insights into ways to focus on resilience and learning across sectors, explore practical application of the learning, and finally focus on the way forward and the implications of what this may mean for leaders of the future.

The whole-life exploration of leadership resilience is embedded throughout this book – in the way that it is written and the inclusion of the whole life of the author and of the findings from studying and working with Third-Sector leaders.

The book can be read in the traditional way, but equally, it can be dipped into and out of. For example, you may be particularly interested in exploring the process of and implications of going back to study as a seasoned leader; you may want to jump to exercises to explore your own resilience as a leader; you may be an academic who wants to critique the learning drawn from my research; or you may be a practitioner or trainer looking for new ideas to build on in your work. I hope you find it useful from whichever perspective you approach it from.

Finally, I've kept in mind a quote that Meredith Norwich, Senior Editor at Routledge, recently used, "For an academic book, you are looking to demonstrate that you stand on the shoulders of giants. For a practitioner book, you ARE the giant... But you're not the first giant". At not much over 5 feet tall, I've never thought of myself as any sort of giant, but if my learning can be useful, I'm delighted I can share it in this way. On that same note, I hugely appreciated the true "giants" who have come before me, have supported me, and taught me everything I know – It's a privilege to be able to build on your knowledge.

The Author

You may ask why I decided to write a book on resilience. I must be honest and admit it was from both personal and professional motivations.

I'll start with the personal and give you a bit of my background, which might give a deeper understanding of my motivation and help you explore where my own stance on resilience comes from. I went straight from school to work, did not go to university, and came from a working-class family. I did not know anyone who had a degree or had gone to university. My mother thought I was a success and had a job for life when I went to work in a bank.

I started back to study after moving into the third, or charity sector, working with a project which encouraged women into education, training, and employment. This ethos included the project staff, and I was supported to start my MBA (Master of Business Administration) through distance learning while working full-time. During my studies, my second child was born, and I became a single parent. Working, studying, and bringing up the kids while keeping a roof over our heads became a complex juggling act. Once my studies were finished and the kids were a bit older, I was able to focus on developing my career. It was only later, once my children had grown up and moved on, and my career had got to a stage where I was seen in my field as a sector leader, that I could turn my attention back to studying.

To reflect on why I moved to the Third Sector, to be completely honest, they had a creche at the first project I went to work for. As a struggling young mum, this was a lifeline! It wasn't until I started to understand the sector that I realised that this was an example of an inclusive approach and that my own values and motivations aligned with the way that we worked and the impact we hoped to have. I think there was also a synergy with those we were working with. All women who wanted a better life and more opportunities for their children. Finding a sector that felt like the right place to be, where I could make a difference, is the reason I stayed in this sector for most of my career.

I think the reason I went back to study was the thinking around what sort of a legacy I could leave for the sector from my learning over the almost 20 years working with sector leaders. By giving this thinking some academic rigour, I hoped it would give it the credibility it needed to be recognised and to be a useful resource that I could give back to a sector where I had enjoyed a long and satisfying career – and a lot of support. There was also a personal element of wanting to prove to myself that I could study at this level, and there was a desire to exercise my brain and learn new things as I move into the next stage of life and learning. Writing this book is a way I can now share this learning more widely – and a way to further stretch myself – and have another adventure in a new field!

As a full-time leader, I recognised that I often skimmed the surface of many areas and rarely had a "deep dive" into the thinking behind the theories I've worked to and the evidence I've heard. My journey had involved a fair bit of leadership learning, which I will pick up on throughout the book. I strongly believe you have to "walk the talk", and anything I am advocating, i.e., learning more about leadership, should be something I am continually open to. Learning is truly lifelong!

Although my route to the DBA (Doctor of Administration) possibly started with studying for an MBA, my story to this point of embarking on writing a book and considering my own resilience should probably be picked up from 2016. My husband and I had planned a world trip to mark a new stage of life (he had retired, and I was considering reducing my hours), a mix of trekking, sightseeing, and adventures. A few weeks into the trip, he took ill and ended up being airlifted off a mountain in New Zealand. After being in intensive care, having a lifesaving operation, and a few weeks of convalescing, he was well enough to be flown home. We were then told he had advanced cancer and only six months to live. I nursed him through his final months, which was one of the most challenging times of my life.

In the following year, I went through a phase of being very aware of how "life is short". I had previously lost my younger brother to a heart attack when he was 39, so losing my husband (and my father six months earlier) reinforced this. I realised I was going through a grieving period and fluctuated between wanting to "be a beach bum and travel the world" and throwing myself into my work. I came to understand that the only thing in life that hadn't changed was my work, and that it was a huge source of satisfaction. Bringing people together, peer support, and good practice sharing are all part of who I am and what I do, and I felt I had a legacy to leave before I moved on – but at this stage I wasn't sure what that was.

In this period of self-reflection, I built on the love of running, which I had developed as a coping mechanism when my husband was ill, and I ran my first half marathon. I also went on my first solo holiday. Alongside this, I was sorting out my late husband's estate, which included a croft on an island off the northwest of Scotland. This included the big decision to keep hold of a 200-year-old croft house with the plan to renovate it.

The following year saw plans being made for the renovations but also included finding ways to challenge myself, including learning to ride a motorbike and completing a charity cycle ride across the mountains of

Nepal to help raise funds to build a palliative care unit (I had previously trekked there with my late husband, so it seemed apt). I also took part in a global leadership programme with cultural intelligence at its core, part of which was in Malaysia and I volunteered for the Glasgow Games (leading a team of volunteers at the golf – something I knew nothing about!). Finally, I was delighted to be awarded an OBE (Order of the British Empire) for my services to the voluntary sector and took my now grown-up kids and my mother to the ceremony at the Palace and met the Queen!

Moving on, I was starting to be a bit more settled; island home developments were moving slowly, and my main adventure was to take a group of sector leaders on a leadership exchange with Russian non-governmental organisation (NGO) peers. We then hosted our partners back in the UK. I was also working with my two board positions, the Charity Regulator in Scotland (Office of the Scottish Charity Regulator, OSCR), where I was Vice Chair, and EUCLID Network (a European network for social impact organisations and their leaders), where I was a board member and had been involved since its inception in 2007.

Naivety has played quite a large part in my life, as has serendipity. I feel opportunities present for a reason, and I don't often think through how challenging they might be (from cycling across Nepal to redesigning and renovating a croft house to starting a DBA – and writing a book!). If I'd known what was involved in any of those, I may never have taken the first step. The four stages of learning (Broadwell, 1969) come to mind – maybe I thrive in the unconscious incompetence. In short, the stages are:

1 Unconscious Incompetence: We don't know that we are incompetent (ignorance).
2 Conscious Incompetence: We know that we are incompetent (awareness).
3 Conscious Competence: We are competent if we consciously think about what we are doing (learning).
4 Unconscious Competence: We can do it without thinking about it (mastery).

I now know that once I have taken those first few steps, if it feels like the right road, I become determined to see what is at the end of it!

Learning over this period has been huge. I've always had a real interest in "walking in other's shoes" and "seeing my own world through other's eyes". I'd always said that I wasn't at all academic, and I was sometimes a bit critical of how long research took and how "knowledge exchange" from academia was often one way (from the academics), so I felt I couldn't "talk the talk" unless I "walked the walk" – thus more of the motivation for my studies.

Throughout my studies, I continued to reflect on my own resilience. These times have shown me that life will have ups and downs, but that we CAN bounce back. We must make the most of the good times, keep putting one foot in front of the other (a lesson I learnt from hillwalking), and that taking on a challenge (even when foolhardy) gives confidence and strength. Achievement boosts confidence. Life keeps knocking you down, and the only way forward is to keep getting back up and doing the best you can while the bruises heal.... And to notice the good times!

The Sector

It's important first to give some background and understanding of the sector that the learning and experiences in this book are based on before I go any further. It is referred to by several different titles, including the Third Sector, Voluntary Sector, NGOs (non-governmental organisations), Civil Society, Social Enterprise, and Not for Profit. Throughout this book, the term "Third Sector" will be used. This term was chosen as it was considered the one most used by Chief Officers to describe their sector at the time of the study.

The research I refer to explores the resilience behaviours of Third-Sector leaders in the context of the challenges they faced in their roles. It focused on registered charities with a "Chief Officer" (salaried), who manages paid staff (and often volunteers) as well as reporting to a voluntary board of management. The term "Chief Officer" will be used for the most senior person in the organisation who reports to the board, as a range of titles are used across the sector to define this role (e.g., Executive Director, Chief Executive, Manager, etc.). It should be noted that where literature considered from other sectors uses the term CEO, this term will continue to be used when referring to that specific work. It should also be noted that out with discussions on the study, the term "leader" will be used more generally.

The Third Sector can be seen as different from other sectors in terms of its motivations, its activities, and the fact that it contributes to social good by building social capital in civil society (do Adro & Leitão, 2020; Hyndman, 2017; Murdock, 2010). It is driven by passion, social ethos, and social value (Armstrong & Wright, 2022). Third-Sector organisations exist across the world; they work within legal and regulatory frameworks and often receive some favourable tax benefits (Hyndman, 2017). There are two main overarching support bodies in the sector in Scotland where these studies are based: the Scottish Council for Voluntary Organisations (SCVO), which is the membership organisation for Scotland's charities, voluntary organisations, and social enterprises, and the ACOSVO, which supports sector leaders through peer support, good practice sharing, and leadership development. In addition, a relatively large number of organisations act as "intermediaries" and provide support in specific thematic or specialist areas.

The Charities and Trustee Investment (Scotland) Act 2023 is, at the time of writing, the legislation which underpins the sector. The Office of The Scottish Charity Regulator (OSCR) is a non-ministerial office of the Scottish Government. Its duties include keeping a register of charities and ensuring they meet the "charity test". To meet the "charity test", an organisation's purpose must meet one (or more) of 16 specific charitable purposes, and the organisation must provide public benefit in Scotland or elsewhere.

The Third Sector in Scotland is large and diverse. According to SCVO, in 2023 it comprised over 24,000 registered charities, over 22,000 more informal community organisations, social enterprises, and credit unions, and had a collective annual turnover of over £8 billion. These organisations deliver services and support across almost all facets of daily life, including social care, culture, sport, education, health, housing, equalities, and the environment.

The sector accounts for around 5% of the Scottish Workforce as well as involving more than 1 million volunteers. There is huge variation in terms of the size and scope of individual organisations. For example, only 28% of charities have paid staff, with the remainder being run purely by volunteers, and a small number of large charities account for most of the sector's income.

The wider public is often not aware of the economic impact of the Third Sector and the "professionalism" of its activities. From the Victorian-era model of philanthropy, the sector has grown, changed, modernised, and professionalised. Legal structures have become more varied, and some would argue that the sector has moved towards a more business-like or social enterprise model.

In terms of issues and challenges facing the sector, SCVO's 2019 Third-Sector Forecast showed that charities would face a financially challenging future. Their survey showed that 34% of charities thought their individual finances would get worse, and 75% of charities thought the financial situation for the whole sector would get worse. It stated that 100% are concerned about rising overheads, and 58% of charities think expenditure will go up compared to 37% who think income will increase. To compound the financial challenges, 81% believe more people will need their services in 2019, leaving organisations in the incredibly difficult situation of trying to respond to an increase in demand with less capacity and resources. The same survey showed the top four challenges for charities in 2019 as: planning for the future, sourcing funding, meeting demand, and proving their worth to funders and the public.

A "charity risk barometer" set up in 2020 by an academic partnership (Ecclesiastical, 2020a) stated that even before the pandemic there were challenges with austerity, attracting talent to the sector, and the instability of the political environment. It showed that the pandemic increased demand for services alongside a decrease in income. It also suggested that the sector had adapted well, rose to the challenge, and developed greater resilience. The report suggested that at this stage, charities were focused more on survival than long-term planning, that there was a risk of employee burnout, and that the ability to adapt was key to that survival.

The Third Sector is a key part of the Scottish Government's strategy for inclusive economic growth and its focus on a well-being economy, in 2022 quoting, "Our vision for Scotland is to transition to a well-being economy: that is, an economic system, within safe environmental limits, which serves and prioritises the collective wellbeing of current and future generations". The sector plays a role in working towards the outcomes in the National Performance Framework (Scottish Government, 2017), which are linked to the global agenda outlined in the United Nations' sustainable development goals (SDGs, United Nations, 2015). Inclusive growth approaches recognise that high levels of inequality weaken economic performance, and the Third Sector is seen as a key player in addressing that inequality.

That being said, the sector still needs greater recognition of the role it plays in society, and many argue that it must be treated as a genuine partner, deserving of an equal place at the table and an operating environment that allows it to deliver to its full potential (SCVO, 2020).

Although the COVID-19 pandemic has had huge implications for the sector and highlighted some of its strengths and weaknesses, this book will have a wider scope and will not focus specifically on that period. However, it would be remiss to not consider the implications and impact of the situation at the time of the research.

During the early days of the pandemic, two in five charities reported an increase in demand for their services, 30% predict an income drop, and 70% believe there will be cuts to budgets as well as services. This has led to half of Third-Sector organisations facing the prospect of running out of funds and possible closure. Over the first six months, the most pressing issues shifted from initial concerns about meeting immediate need, securing funding, and dealing with limited digital and staffing capacity to current concerns about financial sustainability, adapting services for long-term change, and "building back better" (SCVO, 2020).

From a wider UK perspective, 94% of charities were worried about the impact of the recession on their finances, 55% feared not being able to meet demand for their services over winter, and 52% had seen public donations fall because of COVID-19. In addition, 47% had revised down their financial forecasts, and 43% were cutting jobs, with the biggest cuts falling in service delivery roles (Martin & Kenley, 2020). The picture painted by these statistics was one of a sector struggling to survive. Emergency funding had been put in place for some organisations, providing short-term support, but the long-term impacts on the sector and the increasing demands these would make on its leaders were still to be fully understood. **The implications could be that the increased demands these challenges place on the leadership of the sector could lead to an increased risk of burnout and have a negative impact on their resilience.**

Health and Safety Executive ((2021) figures state that 822,000 workers across all sectors were suffering from work-related stress, anxiety, or depression. An estimated 449,000 employees report that their symptoms have been made worse by the effects of the pandemic. The corporate cost of mental health-related absences and lost productivity to UK businesses in 2020 is estimated at £14 billion (Westfield Health, 2021). By March 2022, a project to measure the "temperature", where temperature is seen as how "hot" or challenging the circumstances are, of the voluntary sector during the pandemic highlighted "diverse and complex experiences" for the sector and thus its leaders (Ecclesiastical, 2020b).

So, the scene has been set, and it seems that resilience is more important than ever for sector leaders during these challenging times. This next section will explore these challenges in a bit more detail before moving on to the study, which will underpin the findings on what keeps leaders resilient.

Why Now – Leadership Challenges

Commentators on current times talk about an "age of bewilderment" in which stories of the past are no longer relevant and stories of the future are yet to evolve (Harari, 2018). With so much change in all spectrums of life, from political, to personal to professional, the speed of change has never been so fast and will never be so slow again (Trudeau, 2018). In the context of sector leadership, Kate Raworth (2017), author of Doughnut Economics, has identified a shift in perspective from growth economics, where success as a leader is about financial success and measures of Gross Domestic Product, to much wider measures of success such as SDGs. This change is reflected at the individual level according to Dhingra et al. (2021), who identified that employees expect their jobs to bring a significant sense of purpose to their lives or they risk losing those employees and the skills they bring to the role. To this extent, the sector could be well placed to hold on to talent if the assertion of increased sense of purpose holds true.

Chief Officers must deal with all the challenges discussed in the previous section whilst also running complex organisations with multiple

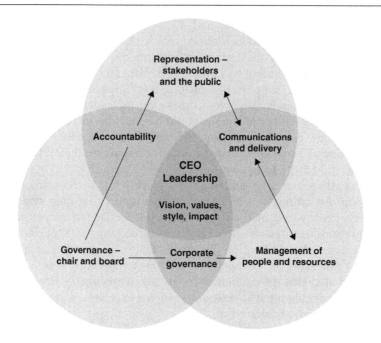

Figure 1.1 The Complexity of Third-Sector Leadership.

Note: A diagram showing three circles intertwined and the role of CEO Leadership (Vision, Values, Style, Impact) at the intersection. The circles show Governance (chair and board), Management (of people and resources), and Representation (stakeholders and the public).

Between governance and representation is accountability.

Between representation and management is communication and delivery.

Between governance and management is corporate governance.

stakeholders, funders, and regulators. The three leadership spheres of a Third-Sector CEO or Chief Officer (Kirchner, 2007), detailed in Figure 1.1 above, show the complexity of the role and the multiple areas that Third-Sector Leaders have to work across.

In his evidence to the House of Lords Select Committee (2017, p. 31), Professor John Mohan from the Third-Sector Research Centre described charity leadership as being not unlike "juggling on a unicycle".

The term VUCA (volatile, uncertain, chaotic, ambiguous) is a long-established descriptor of operating environments and is particularly relevant to the Third Sector. Bill George, Professor of Management Practice at Harvard, noted that the pressures this environment creates require leaders to respond with vision, understanding, clarity, and adaptability (George, 2018).

Evidence of increasing pressure on the leaders in the sector due to increased demand, reduced funding, increased competition, and an environment of constant change pre-dates COVID-19 (do Adro & Leitão, 2020). Leaders must ensure that they continuously innovate, evidence impact, and stand up to the scrutiny of both stakeholders and the public. These challenges can lead to a heightened risk of stress and burnout and ultimately individuals standing down as Chief Officer or even leaving the sector entirely. This was evidenced in a study, Path to Impact, which explored the capacity of 100 Third-Sector organisations and found that "succession planning" and "re-energising" were particularly problematic areas (RF Associates, 2018). As a sector with such importance both economically and socially for the well-being of our nation, the issues of resilience and risk of burnout from its leaders are crucially important.

The Third Sector's lack of capacity and resources can exacerbate the "normal" challenges of leadership. A 2019 study found that Third-Sector leaders work three months of the year for free, doing an average of ten hours per week over and above their paid role (ACEVO, 2019). This style of habitually working beyond capacity is clearly unsustainable, with previous research demonstrating that overloading the brain can have negative impacts, including causing anxiety (Gruszka & Nęcka, 2017; Kirsh, 2000).

Allcock Tyler (2017) suggests that Third-Sector leadership is a vocation, not a profession. This widely held perception can make the leadership role even more complex to navigate, adding a more personal and emotional element to leaders' "obligations" alongside the expected drive for excellence, growth, and high performance as well as value for money and evidence of impact. The fact that they have line managers who are volunteers and may not have experience in this area and that the Chief Officer is expected to support the board as well as being supported and often line managed by board members, could also increase the complexity.

Survey results from Charity Works Impact Research (Jones, 2019) demonstrated that Chief Executives working in the charity sector in England are experiencing high levels of stress. Seventy-two percent of Chief Executives reported feeling stressed in their role at present, with 18% of respondents saying they felt "very stressed" and 54% saying they felt "quite stressed". There was no correlation found between levels of stress and the length of time that a Chief Executive had been in their current role. Similarly, 87% of respondents reported experiencing one or more symptoms of burnout. The most common symptoms were difficulty concentrating and suffering from insomnia, with 64% of respondents reporting these symptoms. A further 61% of respondents reported they were suffering from anxiety, and 55% said they were experiencing reduced performance. Research in the Health and Social Care field has found that new leadership positions can be overwhelming when leaders are asked to work in new areas and across sectors, as is becoming increasingly the case (Elliott, 2020).

These unique factors affecting leadership in the Third Sector all mean that corporate styles of leadership often do not work as intended. It is therefore pertinent to exercise caution when applying much of the existing academic literature, which focuses almost exclusively on the public and private sectors, to this context.

Studies have demonstrated that individuals experiencing burnout reduce their job involvement and organisational commitment (Lee & Ashforth, 1996), which can negatively affect performance (Maslach et al., 2001). Consequently, CEO burnout is not only detrimental to the CEO's well-being but can adversely affect the performance of the organisation.

Research to date has shown that much of the current focus is on workforce well-being, and there is generally a lack of focus on CEO well-being (Barling & Cloutier, 2016). There is mounting pressure on leaders to perform well in an increasingly complex and unpredictable context (Jones, 2019). There is an increased need for sustainable leadership to cope with increased demand for services and support (Gerard et al., 2017).

It became apparent that any research in this area in current times needed to consider the pressures on the sector and on its leaders. Studies had to be visibly simple to take part in and of benefit to the sector and its leaders in order to gain both uptake and credibility. The accessibility of the approach was aligned with the rigour of the research to reach the desired aim: "to explore behaviours" which may influence and improve resilience for Third-Sector leadership. The aim of writing this book is to disseminate the learning and my experiences more widely and to connect with other sectors to see what learning can be shared.

With the risk of burnout being high (ACOSVO, 2021), it is imperative that leaders understand the behaviours that support their resilience and are encouraged to take time to consider what works best for them and ensure that they can practice those behaviours in their everyday lives. It is crucial therefore that this research consider both knowledge and practice-based perspectives.

This "whole life" or holistic look at leadership resilience aligns with my own view that the values across personal and professional lives of Third-Sector leaders, what drew them to the sector, and the motivation and the drive to make a difference all coalesce into who we are and how we work. Although it may mean that we are at a higher risk of burnout, I would argue that it also means we have had to become more resilient and draw from all parts of our lives to do so.

Going forward, this book will draw from my doctoral studies, which "explored behaviours which may influence and improve resilience for third sector leaders" (Armstrong, 2023) and consider the wider implication and potential for learning across all sectors.

Summary

This chapter considered the concept of leadership resilience, gave an overview of my own resilience journey as the author and an insight into what led me to write this book. It gives an overview of the Third Sector in Scotland where my study and experiences were based. It introduced the reasoning for the topic I chose for my academic research, which validates the learning. It also introduces why the changing world of work impacts my findings and why the Third Sector could be seen as leading the way in this thinking on leadership resilience in today's fast-changing world. The next chapter will now introduce the research and give an overview of background and subject matter.

Resilience Reflections & Analogy

We make plans and the gods laugh.... This is how I felt when my world turned upside down while on my world trip, but also at different levels throughout my time as a leader. We never know what is around the corner; we can only make a best guess based on our knowledge, experience, and gut instinct.

What we must focus on is our own resilience while navigating through the unexpected changes. We can only be the best version of ourselves if we pay heed to how we feel, understand what keeps us resilient, and look at it through a whole-life, holistic perspective that this book will help you explore.

References

ACEVO. (2019). *Pay and Equalities Survey 2019: This Year the Average Charity CEO will Spend Three Months Working for No Pay–ACEVO.* https://www.acevo. org.uk/2019/03/pay-and-equalities-survey-2019-this-year-the-average-charity-ceo-will-spend-three-months-working-for-no-pay/

ACOSVO. (2021). *Wellbeing, Succession & Diversity in Scotland's Voluntary Sector Leadership.* ACOSVO. https://acosvo.org.uk/resources/wellbeing-succession

Allcock Tyler, D. (2017). *Directory of Social Change – Publications.* Directory of Social Change. https://www.dsc.org.uk/publications/

Armstrong, P. (2023). *Fired Up, Not Burnt Out: An Exploration of Resilience Behaviours in Third Sector Leadership* [Edinburgh Napier University]. https://doi.org/10.17869/enu.2023.3170309

Armstrong, P., & Wright, M. (2022). Governance in the Charity/Voluntary Sector. In *A Director's Guide to Governance in the Boardroom across the Private, Public and Voluntary Sectors* (pp. 393–418). Taylor & Francis Ltd. ISBN: 9780367696801

Barling, J., & Cloutier, A. (2016). Leaders' Mental Health at Work: Empirical, Methodological, and Policy Directions. Journal of Occupational Health Psychology, 22(3), 394–406. https://doi.org/10.1037/ocp0000055

Broadwell, M. m. (1969). Teaching For Learning (XVI.). *Gospel Guardian, 20*(41), 1-3a. https://www.wordsfitlyspoken.org/gospel_guardian/v20/v20n41p1-3a.html

Dhingra, N., Samo, A., Schaninger, B., & Schrimper, M. (2021). *Help your Employees Find Purpose-Or Watch them Leave.* McKinsey & Company. https://www.mckinsey.com/business-functions/people-and-organizational-performance/our-insights/help-your-employees-find-purpose-or-watch-them-leave

do Adro, F. J. N., & Leitão, J. C. C. (2020). Leadership and Organizational Innovation in the Third Sector: A Systematic Literature Review. *International Journal of Innovation Studies, 4*(2), 51–67. https://doi.org/10.1016/j.ijis.2020.04.001

Ecclesiastical. (2020a). *Charity Risk Barometer 2020.* https://www.ecclesiastical.com/insights/charity-risk-barometer-2020/

Ecclesiastical. (2020b). *Charity Risk Barometer 2020 | Ecclesiastical.* https://www.ecclesiastical.com/insights/charity-risk-barometer-2020/

Elliott, I. C. (2020). The Implementation of a Strategic State in a Small Country Setting—The Case of the 'Scottish Approach.' *Public Money and Management, 40*(4), 285–293. https://doi.org/10.1080/09540962.2020.1714206

George, B. (2018). *VUCA 2. 0: A Strategy for Steady Leadership In An Unsteady World.* 2–5. https://www.forbes.com/sites/hbsworkingknowledge/2017/02/17/vuca-2-0-a-strategy-for-steady-leadership-in-an-unsteady-world/#271a8a4013d8

Gerard, L., McMillan, J., & D'Annunzio-Green, N. (2017). Conceptualising Sustainable Leadership. *Industrial and Commercial Training.* https://doi.org/10.1108/ICT-12-2016-0079

Gruszka, A., & Nęcka, E. (2017). Limitations of Working Memory Capacity: The Cognitive and Social Consequences. *European Management Journal, 35*(6), 776–784. https://doi.org/10.1016/j.emj.2017.07.001

Harari, Y. N. (2018). *21 Lessons for the 21st Century.* Penguin Random House.

Health and Safety Executive. (2021). Work-Related Stress, Anxiety or Depression Statistics in Great Britain, 2021. *Annual Statistics,* 1–9. https://www.hse.gov.uk/statistics/lfs/index.htm

House of Lords Select Committee. (2017). *HOUSE OF LORDS Select Committee on Charities Report of Session 2016-17 Stronger Charities for a Stronger Society.* https://publications.parliament.uk/pa/ld201617/ldselect/ldchar/133/13302.htm

Hyndman, N. (2017). The Charity Sector: Changing Times, Changing Challenges. *Public Money & Management, 37*(3), 149. https://doi.org/10.1080/09540962.2017.1281608

Jones, V. (2019). The Wellbeing of Chief Executives in the Charity Sector. *Charityworks Impact Research.*

Kirchner, A. (2007). A Leadership Model for Export. *International Journal of Leadership in Public Services, 3*(3), 49–55. https://doi.org/10.1108/17479886200700021

Kirsh, D. (2000). A Few Thoughts on Cognitive Overload. *Intellectica. Revue de l'Association Pour La Recherche Cognitive.* https://doi.org/10.3406/intel.2000.1592

Lee, R. L., & Ashforth, B. E. (1996). A Meta-Analytic Examination of the Correlates of the Three Dimensions of Job Burnout. *Journal of Applied Psychology, 81*(2), 123–133. https://doi.org/10.1037/0021-9010.81.2.123

Martin, A., & Kenley, A. (2020). *PBE Covid Charity Tracker Results in partnership with Charity Finance Group and the Institute of Fundraising.* https://www.ons.gov.uk/employmentandlabourmarket/peopleinwork/earningsandworkinghours/bulletins/ear

Maslach, C., Schaufeli, W. B., & Leiter, M. P. (2001). Job Burnout. *Annual Review of Psychology, 52,* 397–422. https://doi.org/10.1146/annurev.psych.52.1.397

Murdock, A. (2010). The Challenge of Leadership for the Third Sector. *The New Public Leadership Challenge,* 300–324. https://doi.org/10.1057/9780230277953_19

Raworth, K. (2017). *Doughnut Economics: Seven Ways to Think Like a 21st-Century Economist.* Random House Business Books.

RF Associates. (2018). *Path to Impact Final Report.* Prepared by RF Associates Acknowledgements. https://acosvo.org.uk/resources/path-to-impact

Scottish Government. (n.d.). *National Performance Framework | National Performance Framework.* 2017. Retrieved October 15, 2020, from https://nationalperformance.gov.scot/

SCVO. (2020). *Supporting Scotland's Vibrant Voluntary Sector Coronavirus and its Impact on the Scottish Voluntary Sector – What Do We Know So Far?* https://storage.googleapis.com/scvo-documents-evidence/0693z00000AuvcFAAR-CoronavirusSurveys_May2020_8Jun.pdf

Trudeau, J. (2018). *No Title.* World Economic Forum, Davos. Retrieved May 9, 2022, from https://www.youtube.com/watch?v=fTl1YNTNb0g

United Nations. (2015). Transforming Our World: The 2030 Agenda for Sustainable Development. United Nations Sustainable Knowledge Platform. *Sustainable Development Goals.* https://sdgs.un.org/goals

Westfield Health. (2021). *Coping with Covid: The Hidden Cost to Businesses (and their people).* https://www2.deloitte.com/content/dam/Deloitte/uk/Documents/consultancy/

Chapter 2

The Research – *Can't See the Wood from the Trees*

Introduction

So now we have the context set, and the real work begins – The Research.

In this chapter, I'll start by saying a bit about what it was like to go back to studying after 20 plus years in the field as a Chief Officer heading up the leadership support body for Third-Sector leaders (ACOSVO, Association of Chief Officers of Scottish Voluntary Organisations). I'll then go on to give an overview of the journey to my findings, both as a leader and as an academic.

My Journey to Becoming an Academic

The juggling of work, life, and study began in October 2019. It was always a busy time workwise with our annual conference and AGM (Annual General Meeting) to focus on at that time of year in the day job as well as starting up full-time doctoral studies. I told my 85-year-old mum what I was up too; she seems to think I am mad to be back studying on top of everything else but seems very proud of her mad daughter too!

My first week at the university was overwhelming. It felt like a strange foreign language was being spoken, and I was very much out of my depth. After being seen as an expert in my field, I was suddenly a student with no understanding of what I was supposed to do.

I had to consider what being a practitioner researcher meant, and at that stage, I wasn't sure if it was a good or a bad thing. I was reminded of the phrase "You don't know what you don't know" (Rumsfeld, 2002) and the definition of intelligence, "knowing how much you don't know" (I think I was just to try to convince myself I wasn't lacking too much)!

The focus on the theoretical underpinning and research philosophy was a bit overwhelming at first, especially the language, which felt quite alien. I was heartened when getting feedback in a session that I might have found a "sweet spot" in terms of the research not having been done before.

DOI: 10.4324/9781032627212-3

I had an interview for a paid board chair position, which would have meant I could have moved from my full-time job to a portfolio career earlier than planned and thus have more time for my studies. I attended the interview on my way back from my island home and had a call as I went through the door to say my younger sister's recently diagnosed cancer was terminal and she wasn't doing well – I totally fluffed the interview as my focus was elsewhere.

Early 2020, I started thinking longer term, reducing work hours to four days a week to allow a day for study time, planning to cut to less again in 2021, and in 2022 finishing work and studies to move to new adventures. Things were moving in other areas of life too, one being discussions with structural engineers and builders to get the island renovation project started. My sister soon moved to a hospice, and I spent most of my spare time there.

I took to printing articles to take to the hospice to read while my sister slept. She sadly passed away on 13th Feb with me, her husband, and kids beside her. It was the same hospice where my husband had died in almost four years earlier, so it was not an easy time to go back through that journey again. It felt like resilience was a very apt topic to be researching. A surprise delivery of flowers arrived the day after my sister died. I presumed they were condolence flower and didn't realise it was Valentine's Day. They were from a guy I had dated a while before who seemed nice, but it had been a bit soon for me, and I had ended it before it got serious. It turned out he had recently moved to my home city, didn't know about my sister, and had never forgotten me – more later… but another (pleasant) distraction from studies.

I also had the annual two-day sector expo (The Gathering), which included being interviewed on stage, breakfast with the First Minister, and then back to helping plan my sister's funeral. My grown-up kids travelled home for the funeral, and it was nice for them to be with me. Hugs from my daughter, and my son fixing things on my car was just what I needed. I started working on my assignment, but I was not in the best place and struggling with the technical aspects.

So, back to my studies; I had decided to take a social constructivist approach. This interpretive approach and the idea of multiple lives/truths resonated with me and my subject matter. I started to focus on what stops Third-Sector CEOs from burning out. A phrase stuck in my mind from a panel chat on philosophical stance: "Research is a series of decisions that have to be justified".

My supervisor suggested I had to be quite selfish to carve out the time to study on a day that I had booked a yoga session. I had the dichotomy of trying to work out what was more "selfish". Taking time to fill my "beaker of resilience" (more on this later), through yoga, or cancelling my class to be selfish about study time.

Helpful comments from my academic supervisors included: "keep it simple, own it, it's your analysis and research, it's okay to do it your way. It is learning a new language, but what you say is your choice, your own interpretation".

At the end of the week, I presented to the study group. I was a bit nervous (not like me), but it went well. I felt I was relatively on par with others and got good feedback on my presentation – both gave me confidence to continue. An interesting discussion on my stance considered what outcome would make me feel satisfied. Do I want to purely understand or to have a practical outcome/contribution? I realised the latter was the case. After some reflection, I also wondered whether my practical leaning has helped my resilience and influenced my wider thinking on the topic. If I can't work something out intellectually, I'll do something practical while my brain works in the background. From my research, I've found I'm not the only one.

And COVID hits!! When starting this journey, none of us could have expected to be working and studying while not allowed out of our homes and to have to change to everything being online overnight. I quickly realise that I must go back up to full-time hours at work to change our delivery model and support the staff, the board, and sector leaders. I work long hours, and getting out means chopping down trees in the garden. I study when I can, but it feels less important in the enormity of what is happening. I take the brave step of "new man" moving in with me to share the journey.

My next achievement was that my island planning application was approved!! Shame I couldn't get anywhere near it to start the work!

So, enough about me and my own resilience – back to my research in its early stages. As a quick reminder, if the academic depth isn't what you are looking for at this stage, feel free to skim the bits of interest or skip to later sections. This book is meant to be used in a way that suits you at whichever stage in your leadership or academic journey.

The Research

I was now about to determine my methodology, embark on my literature review, and set the scene for the way forward. This next section will give an insight into my exploration of the topic, the methodology I worked within, and the conceptual framework I ultimately chose as a comparator for the research. For those of you about to embark on a research journey, this may give an insight into the process that underpins the work to be done. For those of you keen to find out the results of the research, this may be of interest to validate and underpin the findings – or may even inspire you to consider your own research in the future.

Methodology

The golden thread, or underpinning ethos, which runs through the research comes from a balance of the researcher's natural stance aligned with the approach most suited to both this type of study and the sector it is set in.

It takes the view that a research strategy should respects the differences between people and the objects of the natural sciences to grasp the subjective meaning of social action (Alan Bryman & Bell, 2011). This research will not predict and explain the characteristics of resilient leadership but will aim to understand the behaviours that contribute to it. It will consider current theories and frameworks and potentially develop new thinking and a reconceptualised framework to contribute to knowledge as well as practice.

A social constructivist, interpretive approach was used, which aligned with the method of semi-structured interviews and the "no one truth" approach that resilience is a concept which means something different to each individual.

For those interested in the methodology of the research:

- The ontological position was constructivist/subjective (Alan Bryman & Bell, 2011).
- The epistemological position was interpretivist (Denzin & Lincoln, 2011).
- The research approach/design was qualitative (Blaikie & Priest, 2019).
- The method was semi-structured interviews (Blaikie & Priest, 2019; Denzin & Lincoln, 2011; Kvale, 2007).

The analysis was themed using an emergent approach.

Summary of Literature Review

Research to date has shown that much of the current focus is on workforce well-being, and there is generally a lack of focus on CEO well-being (Barling & Cloutier, 2017). There is mounting pressure on leaders to perform well in an increasingly complex and unpredictable context (Jones, 2019). There is an increased need for sustainable leadership to cope with increased demand for services and support (Gerard et al., 2017).

In current times, with the risk of burnout being high, (ACOSVO, 2021), it is imperative that leaders understand the behaviours that support their resilience and are encouraged to take time to consider which behaviours work best for them and ensure that they can practice those behaviours in their everyday lives. It is crucial, therefore, that the research considers both knowledge and practice-based perspectives. The aim of the research was thus to explore behaviours which may influence and improve resilience for Third-Sector leadership.

To set boundaries for the study, interview participants were leaders of organisations based in Scotland with over £500K turnover and registered as charities. Subjects were all currently Chief Officers or, if a UK organisation, the most senior person in Scotland. The position of leaders, i.e., Chief Officers, was chosen as the focus group for this study. The Oxford Dictionary (2022) states that leadership is "The action of leading a group of people or an organisation" rather than the position, but those in this position are the subjects whose resilience is impacted on through this act; thus, Chief Officers were the participants chosen for this study.

Although charities registered in Scotland was a parameter for this research, and it could be argued that Scots see the world in a particular way (Craig, 2011), it was hoped that the findings would be more widely applicable.

It had also become apparent that any research in this area in current times needed to consider the pressures on the sector and on its leaders. Studies had to be visibly simple to take part in and of benefit to the sector and its leaders in order to gain both uptake and credibility. The research took an interpretive approach and was based on semi-structured interviews. The first stage was to consider the existing literature.

Resilience is defined in many ways. The Cambridge dictionary states that it is:

> the ability to be happy, successful, etc. again after something difficult or bad has happened: Trauma researchers emphasize the resilience of the human psyche. The quality of being able to return quickly to a previous good condition after problems: the capacity to recover quickly from difficulties; toughness.
>
> (Cambridge University Press, 1995)

Bagi (2013) defines burnout as the point at which the person's ability to function is severely impaired.

The Resilience Dynamic (Campbell, 2019) defines resilience as one's ability to adapt and capacity for change. It includes coping and bounce-back:

> the capability of a strained body to recover its size and shape after deformation caused especially by compressive stress.an ability to recover from or adjust easily to misfortune or change.

For the purpose of the study, resilience was defined as the ability to bounce back after a setback, as implied above.

The topic of resilience did not fit neatly into one discipline. There is much research in this area within the fields of work and leadership, which is explored in detail by Ledesma (2014), but less research that looks specifically at the Third Sector. The context, governance, and management of the Third Sector all mean that there could be specific differences in the resilience of leaders, so sector-specific data and research were seen to be key to a deeper understanding of the questions, the findings, and the potential impact of the study.

This wide lens of leadership is explored first through The Handbook of Leadership (Bryman et al., 2011), who suggest that leadership is a key part of organisational and social life and that the study of leadership has never been more widespread and in-depth.

The four different ways that leadership is traditionally understood were then considered through the thinking of Grint and Smolovic-Jones (2005). They assert that leadership can be seen as:

- Who they (they leader) are as a person.
- What they achieve.
- Where they operate.
- How they get things done.

This thinking suggests that there is a multidisciplinary consideration to be taken when exploring leadership – and it is not only one approach, truth, or action that defines it.

In my study, both the act and the position were incorporated. The participants of the study held recognised leadership positions as Chief Officers, but the focus was on the resilience behaviours that they identified while in the act of leading.

In the history of organisational psychology, Maslow (1943) explored a theory of human motivation which most readers will be familiar with. His work showed that basic physiological needs must be met before psychological needs could be reached. He defined these "higher" needs as safety and security, social satisfaction and belongingness, ego and self-esteem, and self-actualisation and personal growth.

Motivations in the Third Sector could arguably be seen in a different way, with the need for achievement and belongingness linked to doing good for others and having a wider impact potentially meaning more than career success and individual wealth. Maslow's content theory of motivation explores the question of "what specific needs cause motivation". This is opposed to a process theory of motivation, which would explore how behaviour is stimulated, directed, sustained, or stopped. If motivation is a factor in resilience and the motivations for working in the sector come from a need to belong and to make a difference, then Maslow's literature may not be as relevant here. Continuing with historical literature on organisational behaviour, Herzberg (1957) explored the content theory through "motivator hygiene", examining the reasons given for positive or negative job satisfaction. He found that hygiene factors such as pay, work environment, and job security only got employees part of the way to being satisfied in their roles. Motivators such as the work itself, challenges, achievement, and responsibility were also necessary to be satisfied in the role. These findings are more in line with the context and motivators of the leaders taking part in this study.

Before moving to the key authors and works in this area, some wider contemporary literature was explored. Duckworth (2016) explored the concept of "grit" as being the "power of passion and persistence". She developed a theory of the psychology of achievement based on a "grit scale", which scored on perseverance and passion.

Cultural Intelligence, or CI, was also explored (Middleton, 2016). As the "successor" of IQ (Stern, 1914) and EQ (Goldman, 2007), CI has been defined by Middleton as the necessary way of thinking for leaders to thrive in the current environment. CI is described as "the ability to cross the divides and thrive in multiple cultures". If this is the case, in the current cross-sectoral world that Third-Sector leaders navigate, this could be another factor that impacts their resilience.

In Dare to Lead (Brown, 2018), Brown's seven-year study looking at the future of leadership posited that courage is a collection of four skill sets that can be taught, observed, and measured (rumbling with vulnerability, living into our values, braving trust, and learning to rise).

Although a wide range of research in the Third Sector does exist, it is often sector-specific and out of the normal business school context of most other sectors. The sector has the added complexity of closeness to identity and passion for a cause. Burnout is more likely if leaders have a blurred line between their work and personal self-identity (Bagi, 2013; Casserley & Megginson, 2009), so it could be argued that this may be more prevalent in the Third Sector. Portnoy (2011) suggests that burnout is not dissimilar to compassion fatigue, a term often used in reference to healthcare workers but which could be used for Third-Sector leaders who see their role as caring for their beneficiaries, their colleagues, and their organisation.

The sector is also complicated by its governance structure. Generally, Third-Sector organisations do not have a "shareholder board" of experienced business leaders to guide and support them. This often leads to a complex interdependency with Third Sector boards looking to the chief officer for support, while at the same time "line managing" them to ensure that targets are met and risk registers are considered. Often little support is given to the Chief Officer position, which has been described as a lonely role with little opportunity to show any vulnerability or uncertainty and with a weight of responsibility for the success of the organisation and the support of its staff, volunteers, and beneficiaries (Terry et al., 2021).

Previous studies and publications on sustainable or resilient leadership have commonly focused on exploring the impact on the organisation in terms of its sustainability or resilience, not the leaders themselves and what helps them be resilient as individuals (Székely & Knirsch, 2005). Existing literature almost exclusively considers this issue in private and public sectors, and therefore, I felt caution must be used when generalising their findings to the Third Sector.

In "Learning from Burnout; Developing sustainable leaders and avoiding career derailment", Casserley and Megginson (2008) interviewed 100 leaders and used some of their stories as a way to explain the challenges and explore what worked and what did not in terms of building resilience. They analysed in-depth interviews with 100 "high-flyers" and considered whether burnout is no longer an unusual event but has become part of a normal lifecycle. They explored 25 years of research, which mainly considered burnout as being a work-related phenomenon which is most likely to affect those early in their career. Their work explored the paradigm of leadership development and considered a new paradigm of leadership learning.

The resulting coping dimensions are added below. Sharing with others was the most frequently reported behaviour of high-flyers who do not burn out. The importance of coming together, peer support, and the opportunity to learn from each other will all be factors more closely examined in this research.

Behaviours of highflyers who did not burn out (Table 2.1):

Table 2.1 Coping dimensions and behaviours

Coping dimension	Behaviour
SHARING A willingness to share work experiences with others during high-stress periods	Does not sit and stew on things – talks to people they need to directly to resolve things. Talks situation over with family and friends to get advice from those with more experience; uses this advice to put things in perspective
PROACTIVITY Takes urgent action to resolve existing or anticipated situations that will result in severe stress	Comes up with alternative solutions to problems to stop high stress from happening Focus on controlling what is in their control, including their own behaviour

(Continued)

Table 2.1 (Continued)

Coping dimension	Behaviour
BOUNDARY SETTING Has a mature and realistic understanding of own capability; accurately accesses workload capability of delivering; clear sets of boundaries around this; only flexes these boundaries on the basis of increased time or resources	Sets clear boundaries – faces down those who try to usurp these Assesses the importance of deadlines they are given. Recognises that some are unrealistic or unnecessary. Ask for more time or assistance
WORKING SMARTER Well-developed organisational skills, including the ability to prioritise, delegate, and work towards a clear end point rather than working long hours and sacrificing personal and social activities	Prioritising and goal setting: sets small goals for the next destination and then reviews from there Takes the approach that 80% right is okay; perfection is fantasy
HOPE Visualising how things might be beyond the immediate, harsh reality of the situation	Sees the opportunity in the situation more than the challenge
RENEWING Engaging in activities outside work that are personally renewing	Does exercise and sport Learn what helps them switch off completely Understand they need time to process what is happening

Source: Table adapted by the Author from Casserley and Megginson (2008).

The causes, costs, and prevention of burnout are considered from a global perspective by Bagi (2013). This is one of the few works which does very briefly mention community organisations, but it does not pull out any sector-specific analysis. Bagi considered that effective leaders can be seen as having "superhero" status, which could lead to unrealistic expectations and result in burnout. He identifies burnout as a deep and persistent experience of physical, emotional, and mental exhaustion and explores the Maslach and Jackson's (1981) three-dimensional framework. He defines burnout as being a combination of individual and work issues and explores the link between the personal characteristics that help people become successful leaders with those that contribute to their risk of burnout. When a person's identity becomes too close to work, he asserts that more excessive workloads are taken on and time boundaries are breached. This passion and commitment, when closely identified with work, can lead to a harder "fall" when the role is no longer viable and the leader loses the sense of identity that it brought. He explored "Type A" personalities (motivated and competitive), who are often successful leaders but also have traits of impatience and irritability, which did increase stress and thus lead to more risk of burnout (Kivimäki et al., 1996; Lundberg et al., 2007). His work culminated in offering three suggestions on how leaders can take responsibility and help themselves reduce their risk of burnout:

- Develop a greater sense of self-awareness and a healthy identity.
- Develop greater emotional resilience.
- Practise self-care.

The past, present, and future of burnout were explored by Schaufeli et al. (1997) through looking at the work of a range of scholars. They concluded that the current state of society in terms of pressure, workload, lack of support, and reduction in staffing "(p 254) all means that burnout will continue to be an issue over the coming years. They argue that over the last decade, there has been a vast amount of both "theoretical thinking and empirical research" and that burnout has been "placed successfully on the academic agenda".

They argue that burnout is considered from four general psychological perspectives:

- Social comparison (Buunk & Schaufeli, 1993)
- A general stress theory (Hobfoll & Freedy, 2018)
- Professional self-efficacy (Cherniss, 1980)
- An integration into the transactional model of occupational stress (Cox et al., 1993)

One of the approaches, the Maslach Burnout Inventory (MBI), has provided a common language for those studying burnout, who can now make direct comparisons between their own findings and those of others. It is used to assess professional burnout in human service, education, business, and government professions (but not the Third Sector), assess and validate the three-dimensional structure of burnout, and understand the nature of burnout for developing effective intervention.

The MBI is a psychological assessment tool which uses 22 symptoms of occupational burnout. It was originally developed by Maslach and Jackson (1981) with the goal of assessing an individual's experience of burnout. It only takes ten minutes to complete and measures three dimensions of burnout: emotional exhaustion, depersonalisation, and personal accomplishment.

From the literature review, much work has gone into considering burnout and resilience in leaders, so the question could be asked as to why more is needed. The answer is in relation to the relevance of the research to the specific sector of the study, considering its governance, the way it is managed, and the role that passion for the cause plays. It could be suggested that resilience can be learned and could be considered a muscle that needs to be built and exercised. That there is a recognised inventory to measure burnout that has not previously been used in this sector could be worth further exploration in future studies.

The History of Resilience

Resilience is often seen as the way to mitigate burnout. The Oxford dictionary defines resilience as: "the capacity to recover quickly from difficulties; toughness".

Academic research into resilience started about 40 years ago with pioneering studies by Garmezy (1991), who looked at why some children suffered more than others when going through difficult childhood experiences. He concluded that resilience played a greater part in good mental health than previously thought.

Vanderpol (2002) found that many of the healthy survivors of concentration camps had what he calls a "plastic shield". The shield was comprised of several factors, including a sense of humour. Other core characteristics that helped included the ability to form attachments to others and the possession of an inner psychological space that protected the survivors from the intrusions of abusive others.

Many of the early theories about resilience stressed the role of genetics and considered whether some people are just born resilient, but there is now increasing evidence that it can be learned. Holyoke and Vaillant (1978), observe that within various groups studied during a 60-year period, some people became more resilient over their lifetimes.

Coutu (2002), considered how resilience can help one survive and recover from even the most brutal experiences and suggested that the following practices would improve resilience:

- Face down reality
- Search for meaning
- Continually improvise

He argued that almost all the theories on resilience overlap in three ways. Resilient people possess three characteristics: a staunch acceptance of reality; a deep belief, often buttressed by strongly held values, that life is meaningful; and an uncanny ability to improvise. You can bounce back from hardship with just one or two of these qualities, but you will only be truly resilient with all three. These three characteristics hold true for resilient organisations as well.

The key to building resilience is optimism, argues Seligman (2011), and that people who don't give up interpret setbacks as temporary, local, and changeable, thus feeling less helpless and more able to deal with the situation.

Herrman et al. (2011) found that definitions of resilience have evolved, but it is referred to as positive adaptation, or the ability to maintain or regain mental health despite experiencing adversity. They consider the interaction of resilience with other areas of life, such as relationships and attachments.

The main learning drawn from the writings on resilience is that although burnout is being explored from a professional, work-life issue, resilience could be seen as more holistic and related to personality, characteristics, experiences, and learning. This will inform the development of thinking in this study going forward.

The idea that leaders should pay attention to their own healthy selfish needs as a pre-requisite of effectiveness was raised by Casserley (2010), whose work proposed an explanation of burnout in which it is the characteristics that are put into play that determine whether a leader is resilient. The study considered an approach that centres on leaders exercising a duty of care for their own sustainability as well as that of the wider business and society.

Casserley and Critchley (2010), building on Casserley and Megginson's (2008) earlier work, felt that their research showed that performance derives from an integration of three core processes:

- Reflection on action (learning through doing).
- Psychological intelligence (having a clear sense of personal purpose and an awareness of personal assumptions and motivations).
- Physiological well-being (effective management of stress and sufficient selfcare).

It is these three core processes and their engagement with the culture of the organisation (shown as a 4th "Hallmark"), which they argue makes for effective leadership development, sustainable leaders, and potentially sustainable organisations.

Research Decision

After completing the literature review, I chose the conceptual framework of "Behaviours of highflyers who did not burn out" as a comparator to consider against the findings of my research with Third-Sector leaders.

Summary

This chapter has explored my research journey and set the scene for the learning that is to follow. It has given an insight into my own resilience during this time and detailed the conceptual framework I will use as a comparator to the findings from my research. The next chapter will go on to give an overview of the findings.

Resilience Reflections and Analogy: Can't See the Wood from the Trees

To me, this analogy is helpful both from thinking about the overview of the research and also around how we view resilience. For some, it's intrinsically linked to the resilience of the organisation, but I focused on what it means for each individual and how it's different for each and every one of us. When we are in amongst it all, being passionate about making a difference in the world, getting through each day, where is the space and time to think about our own resilience? The aim was to focus in on this aspect and find answers which might help us all, as leaders, think about our resilience and what keeps us getting up to fight another day. Remembering that it is unique to each of us, we can find ways of exploring solutions that work for us so that we can rise up to see the overview of the forest, but still be clear about what each of us needs as an individual "tree".

References

ACOSVO. (2021). *Wellbeing, Succession & Diversity in Scotland's Voluntary Sector Leadership*. ACOSVO. https://acosvo.org.uk/resources/wellbeing-succession

Bagi, S. (2013). When Leaders Burn Out: The Causes, Costs and Prevention of Burnout among Leaders. *Advances in Educational Administration, 20*, 261–289. https://doi.org/10.1108/S1479-3660(2013)0000020015

Barling, J., & Cloutier, A. (2017). Leaders' Mental Health at Work: Empirical, Methodological, and Policy Directions. *Journal of Occupational Health Psychology, 22*(3), 394–406. https://doi.org/10.1037/ocp0000055

Blaikie, N., & Priest, J. (2019). Designing Social Research (3rd ed.). Polity Press.

Brown, B. (2018). *Dare to Lead*. Vermilion.

Bryman, A., & Bell, E. (2011). Business Research Methods -. In Business Research Method (3rd ed.). Oxford University Press.

Bryman, A., Collinson, D., Grint, K., Jackson, B., & Uhl-Bien, M. (2011). *Handbook of Leadership*. Sage.

Buunk, B. P., & Schaufeli, W. B. (1993). Burnout: A Perspective from Social Comparison Theory. *APA Psycnet*.

Cambridge University Press. (1995). *Cambridge Dictionary*. https://dictionary.cambridge.org/

Campbell, J. (2019). *The Resilience Dynamic*. Practical Inspiration Publishing.

Casserley, T. (2010). Learning from Burnout. *Human Resource Management International Digest, 18*(1). https://doi.org/10.1108/hrmid.2010.04418aae.001

Casserley, T., & Critchley, B. (2010). A New Paradigm of Leadership Development. *Industrial and Commercial Training, 42*(6), 287–295. https://doi.org/10.1108/00197851011070659

Casserley, T., & Megginson, D. (2008). Learning from Burnout. In Learning from Burnout. https://doi.org/10.4324/9780080942155

Casserley, T., & Megginson, D. (2009). *Learning from Burnout: Developing Sustainable Leaders and Avoiding Career Derailment.* Elsevier. https://doi.org/10.4324/9780080942155

Cherniss, c. (1980). *Professional Burnout in Human Service Organizations.* Praeger.

Coutu, D. L. (2002). How Resilience Works. *Harvard Business Reviewrvard Business Review, 80*(5), 46–56. www.hbr.org

Cox, T., Kuk, G., & Leiter, M. P. (1993). Burnout, Health, Work Stress, and Organizational Healthiness. *APA Psycnet.* https://psycnet.apa.org/record/1993-97794-011

Craig, C. (2011). *Scots Crisis of Confidence.* Argyll Publishing.

Denzin, N., & Lincoln, Y. (2011). The SAGE Handbook of Qualitative Research. SAGE Publications, Ltd.

Duckworth, A. (2016). *Grit.* Vermilion.

Garmezy, N. (1991). Resiliency and Vulnerability to Adverse Developmental Outcomes Associated with Poverty. *American Behavioral Scientist, 34*(4), 416–430. https://doi.org/10.1177/0002764291034004003

Gerard, L., McMillan, J., & D'Annunzio-Green, N. (2017). Conceptualising sustainable leadership. *Industrial and Commercial Training, 49*(3), 116–126. https://doi.org/10.1108/ICT-12-2016-0079

Goldman, D. (2007). *Emotional Intelligence.* Bloomsbury Publishing.

Grint, K., & Smolovic-Jones, O. (2005). *Leadership: Limits and Possibilities.* Palgrave McMillan.

Herrman, H., Stewart, D. E., Diaz-Granados, N., Berger, E. L., Jackson, B., & Yuen, T. (2011). What is Resilience? *Canadian Journal of Psychiatry, 56*(5), 258–265. Canadian Psychiatric Association. https://doi.org/10.1177/070674371105600504

Herzberg, F. (1957). *The Motivation to Work.* John Wiley & Sons.

Hobfoll, S. E., & Freedy, J. (2018). *Conservation of Resources: A General Stress Theory Applied to Burnout* (pp. 115–129). Routledge. https://doi.org/10.4324/9781315227979-9

Holyoke, T. C., & Vaillant, G. E. (1978). Adaptation to Life. *The Antioch Review, 36*(2). https://doi.org/10.2307/4638047

Jones, V. (2019). The Wellbeing of Chief Executives in the Charity Sector. *Charityworks Impact Research.*

Kivimäki, M., Kalimo, R., & Julkunen, J. (1996). Components of Type A Behavior Pattern and Occupational Stressor-Strain Relationship: Testing Different Models in a Sample of Industrial Managers. *Behavioural Medicine, 22*(2), 67–76. https://doi.org/10.1080/08964289.1996.9933766

Kvale, S. (2007). Doing Interviews. SAGE Publications, Ltd. https://doi.org/10.4135/9781849208963

Ledesma, J. (2014). Conceptual Frameworks and Research Models on Resilience in Leadership. *SAGE Open, 4*(3). https://doi.org/10.1177/2158244014545464

Lundberg, U. E., Johansson, G., & Schaufelt, W. B. (2007). Type A Behavior and Work Situation: Associations with Burnout and Work Engagement. *Scandinavian Journal of Psychology, 48*(2), 135–142. https://doi.org/10.1111/j.1467-9450.2007.00584.x

Maslach, C., & Jackson, S. E. (1981). The Measurement of Experienced Burnout. *Journal of Organizational Behavior*, 2(2), 99–113. https://doi.org/10.1002/job. 4030020205

Maslow, A. H. (1943). A Theory of Human Motivation. *Psychological Review*, 50(4), 370–396. https://doi.org/10.1037/h0054346

Middleton, J. (2016). *Cultural Intelligence*. Bloomsbury Academic.

Oxford Dictionary. (2022).

Portnoy, D. (2011). Burnout and Compassion Fatigue-Watch for the Signs. *Journal of the Catholic Health Association of the United States, July-August*, 47–50. https://www.chausa.org/publications/health-progress/archives/issues/july-august-2011/burnout-and-compassion-fatigue-watch-for-the-signs

Rumsfeld, D. (2002). *Pentagon Press Briefing*. https://web.archive.org/web/2016040 6235718/http://archive.defense.gov/Transcripts/Transcript.aspx?TranscriptID= 2636

Schaufeli, W. B., Maslach, C., & Marek, T. (1997). Professional Burnout Recent Developments in Theory and Research. *Accident and Emergency Nursing*, 5(1), 57. https://doi.org/10.1016/s0965-2302(97)90071-0

Seligman, M. E. P. (2011). Building Resilience. *Harvard Business Review*, 89(4), 100–106.

Stern, W. (1914). *The Psychological Methods of Testing Intelligence*. Warwick & York, Inc.

Székely, F., & Knirsch, M. (2005). Responsible Leadership and Corporate Social Responsibility. *European Management Journal*, 23(6), 628–647. https://doi. org/10.1016/j.emj.2005.10.009

Terry, V., Rees, J., & Jacklin-Jarvis, C. (2021). The Difference Leadership Makes? Debating and Conceptualising Leadership in the UK Voluntary Sector. *Voluntary Sector Review*, 11(1), 99–111. Policy Press. https://doi.org/10.1332/20408 0519x15634331938320

Vanderpol, M. (2002). Resilience: A Missing Link in our Understanding of Survival. *Harvard Review of Psychiatry*, 302–306. https://doi.org/10.1080/10673220216282

Chapter 3

Key Findings – *The More You Know, the More You Realise You Don't Know*

Introduction

This chapter takes the reader through the next stage of my research journey. It considers the impact of the pandemic, which leaders across all sectors were finding a strain on their resilience and starts to explore the findings of the research that were starting to take shape. The interview questions of the research are detailed, with a first look at responses which will be analysed further in following chapters. It will conclude with a comparison of the reconceptualised framework and suggest a new concept of "Holistic Leadership Resilience".

Moving Forward as an Academic

I found the Impact of the pandemic on my studies challenging. With no in-person contact I felt more isolated and not being able to go into the university made it harder to be clear about finding separate time for studies. I was also struggling with being there for my elderly parents my mum and my stepdad (they married when I was 12 and I will just refer to as dad in future chapters), who were still reeling from losing my sister. Both became much frailer and needing more support during this time. It was hard for me to be there for them, but I was also very aware of protecting them from COVID by keeping my distance.

I was still finding the balancing act of life, work, and studies a challenge. Managing the renovation of a 200-year-old croft house and, after a surprise proposal, realising that during 2021 I would also be organising a wedding, meant that the juggling act wasn't getting any easier! … Life is short – as I know all too well!

Workwise I was steering the organisation through the pandemic. There was an increased demand for support; we made the decision to move offices, and new staff had to be brought on board. We very quickly had to move to fully online support and delivery. Sometimes I felt the pull of

DOI: 10.4324/9781032627212-4

loyalties in all directions. One phrase I used a lot when supporting leaders dealing with so much change was that "what you do and why you do it (your mission and purpose) doesn't change, only **how** you do it". I'm hoping it made the enormity of the changing times seem a little less daunting.

I also had a big blow when my chairperson suddenly passed away. He had been my supporter, mentor, friend, and external supervisor for my studies – and was the same age as me. We had been working closely together for around eight years, and it was a challenging time. Around the same time, my regulator board chair became sick, and I had to temporarily step up as chair. Supporting my own organisation through this time as well as supporting another board was a big strain on my time and well-being, and studies started to take second (or even third or fourth) place.

When the juggling got too much, I would put things on paper to try to help me feel more in control. I had giant A3 "sticky" notes on my wall, which sometimes resembled a crime scene from a TV show – all showing different lists in each of the areas I was working on (work, board, renovations, wedding, kids, parents, etc.).

By the end of the year, things were on a bit more of an even keel, but I had another blow: my previous Treasurer, who I had cycled across Nepal with for a charity bike ride, passed away suddenly. By December, lockdown rules tightened up, and seeing family became even more of a challenge. Sadly, the final bit of bad news was that my Vice Chair, in his late 50s, had also passed away suddenly. I was ready for this year to end. I know many of us had similar losses to deal with during this time, and resilience was definitely at the forefront of finding a way to keep going.

One positive impact of my research work on my day job was the "intelligence gathering" work that had been inspired by my studies, which we had started early in the pandemic. It was still going strong, getting funded, and allowing us to adapt to members needs much more quickly than previously. It was also of interest to government, and funders in terms of evidencing the impact on the leaders and the wider sector.

I was also asking for help when I struggled with my studies. One colleague with a more academic background helped with tips on structuring and "chunking down", and another gave the sound advice that "it's not some magical other world" and gave me confidence to continue. Once I got going with the writing, I realised I really am "doing it"!! I also read the book with the coping dimensions model that I would go on to use as a basis for comparison (Casserley & Megginson, 2009).

Just after I started carrying out my interviews, I was interviewed myself for a sector "barometer" study. It was helpful to be reminded what it felt like from the "other side of the fence". I also spoke to others who had completed PhDs; hearing how they got through it gave me confidence too. Often, I found there were people I knew who I didn't know were also studying.

One of the girls from my running group was a year ahead in her PHD and gave me some great tips (while running – see Chapter 8 for active leadership).

I spoke at a Third-Sector research forum conference (a window of being able to meet in person), which helped me see myself in this mode and helped my confidence. The DBA (Doctor of Business Administration) group (the cohort studying together) had a catch up, which was always helpful too. I would never underestimate the power of peer support.

Over the summer, I had agreed to do a chapter on the impact of the pandemic on Third-Sector leaders in an academic book, based on case studies and sector research. This was initially advised against by my supervisors as I had so much to do, but I ended up (like earlier in the year when asked to write a chapter on Third-Sector governance) inviting a colleague to co-write with me – always better to do it together. The experience of being peer reviewed and being asked to peer review others was an extremely useful learning experience.

To some extent, I'm sharing my own resilience journey through this research as a sort of unofficial case study, and I'm sure everyone reading this book will have their own experiences from all areas of life that have affected their resilience.

In terms of the resilience behaviours that I exhibited over this period, adaptability was important, as was stability in so much change. Experience counted to give me confidence to keep moving forward, and as ever, my peer support networks kept me going. In terms of mindsets, there was an element of self-belief, knowing what works for me, and hanging on to optimism when things got tough.

So enough about me – back to the research. The next section of this chapter will take you through each question that was asked and an analysis of the responses.

Key Findings: Questions & Responses

With my interviews now set up and ready to go – the questions asked were:

- Can you tell me what resilience means for you in your role as a Third-Sector leader?
- Can you tell me what behaviours you think might have an impact on resilience?
- What do you think improves your resilience and your ability to bounce back after a setback?
- What do you think might help sector leaders more generally in sustaining their resilience?
- What advice would you give to a new leader on their resilience/what would you have done differently with hindsight?

The questions incorporated the consideration that there may be a difference in participants' viewpoints on their own personal resilience, and their view is on what other leaders or the sector in general need in terms of their resilience and behaviours. As the leaders interviewed were all successful and experienced leaders in their field, it was valuable to explore both aspects. This could also be tied to "imposter syndrome" and confidence – whether leaders feel they are less capable in coping with their own resilience compared to others.

Understanding of Resilience

Question 1: Can you tell me what resilience means for you in your role as a Third-Sector leader?

The first question explored how sector leaders understood resilience. It could be argued that the question did not necessarily ask for the participants to explain their understanding more widely, but what resilience meant to them in their role as a leader. This was a decision made from the perspective that the research was not looking for which of the commonly used understandings or definitions of resilience participants could identify, but what resilience really meant for them in practical terms. This aligned to the interpretivist approach of the research and meant that a greater depth of consideration was given to the question.

Understanding Personal Resilience

The themes of **Holistic, Networks,** and **Teams** were raised frequently through the interviews. The discussions considered the balance between personal, organisational, and sectoral resilience and, within this, where support can be found. This included sourcing support both internally within the organisation and externally in the sector or from the wider professional world. The personal understanding themes included

- Holistic/Networks/Teams
- Human/Values/Trust/Impact/Kindness
- Evolving/Moving forward/Adaptability
- Selfcare
- Energy/Limitations/Knowing yourself
- Not taking things personally

One leader's explanation considered "two pots" of resilience and theorised that whilst both the work pot and the home pot could be drawn on at different times, resilience was challenged when both pots were low.

The discussion went on to consider that compartmentalising challenges could be helpful to resilience.

There was consideration that "people stuff" could be a big drain on resilience but could also be a big part of adding to resilience. Some discussed "organisational resilience" and "personal resilience" and the interaction between the two. This was further broken down with examples of areas of work where participants felt they could be very resilient in some and less so in others.

There were also discussions on how resilience meant bringing your team with you, having the right people around you, and having the right networks to support you. The quotes below pull out both of those aspects of teams and networks.

These next themes of **Human, Values, Trust, Impact,** and **Kindness,** come together under the human aspects of leadership and resilience. The leader's values, the importance of trust, the impact they (or their organisation through their leadership) hopes to have, and the kindness they can show and be shown in their role all impact their resilience. Participants found value in acknowledging that the leadership role is difficult but that it can be done with integrity, built around personal ethics, and taking the character of the leaders into account.

Leading in a way that is caring and being able to bring emotions into the situation was also thought to be key to resilience. Resilience was defined by some as sustainability, both in their personal sustainability as a leader and also of their organisation, in that the leader is only as good as they deliver. Impact was included in this theme in the sense of "walking the talk" and modelling organisational and personal values both internally and externally. This related back to participants' understanding of the holistic and human aspects of resilience behaviours.

Some felt that trust, both in oneself and in others, was crucial to resilience. Love, compassion, and kindness, to self, and others, were also mentioned as key behaviours. One participant highlighted that resilience should not be worn "as a badge of honour" in a way that it is expected of leaders to get to that burnt-out state that they must then bounce back from.

From the themes of **Evolving, Moving Forward,** and **Adaptability,** the ability to respond flexibly to change and keep moving forward came through as ways to explain or understand resilience. There was an understanding of the need to keep up with changes and trends as they happen and, if things are not working, of being bold enough to change course.

The term **Self-care** was brought up when addressing the question of how to define resilience. The responses focused on the challenge of looking after oneself when the focus is generally on being a leader, getting the job done, and looking after staff and beneficiaries.

Keeping track and managing one's **Energy** levels and being aware of when **Limitations** are close to being reached came out in several of the interviews as detailed in the following quotes. Being able conserve energy for the end of the day to maintain a good quality of life and cope with tasks outside of work were highlighted as ways of understanding resilience. The importance of **knowing yourself** and what worked for you as a leader underpinned this thinking around resilience.

Another factor which came though on discussions on the leadership role in relation to understanding of resilience was **Not taking things personally**. This was generally characterised by accepting that some things occur out with the leader's responsibility, and that other's behaviours often say more about their own struggles than the action of their leader. (Reynolds et al., 2010).

Understanding Resilience Factors

Some of the responses given could be better described as resilience factors. These aspects were those that were not personal to their leadership role or how they understood resilience for themselves, but more general or organisational aspects of resilience which impacted on their personal resilience. The resilience factors of understanding can be summarised as:

- Information/Experience
- Control/Stabilising/Addressing issues/Focus
- Bounce back

Having the right **Information** and sufficient **Experience** to draw on came to the fore. There was a clear understanding that previous experiences from all parts of life could be drawn on, and that when facing unfamiliar challenges, it is vital to search out information and intelligence to inform confident decision-making.

The themes of **Control, Stabilising, Addressing Issues,** and **Focus** have been grouped together as ways in which some sort of order or control can be taken of a situation. Leaders talked about how they were able to absorb setbacks or unexpected changes and still move towards their goals with some deviation where needed. The discussions detailed how leaders must mould and bend themselves around a problem to find a solution. Some talked about the swanlike (Scamell, 2011) role of appearing steady when others are panicking, whilst some explained it as shielding others and the importance of feeling in control. Finally, some responses spoke of staying focused in spite of distractions or not being undone, even when overwhelmed.

Bounce Back: One of the most used definitions of resilience, "to bounce back after a setback", was purposefully not mentioned by the interviewer in the questions but did come up occasionally in the responses. The reason it wasn't mentioned was so that the respondents were not led by a perceived "correct" definition by the researcher. One participant suggested that resilience could also be stepping into something without a setback, while another felt that their ability to cope with stress, change, or challenge and bounce back was what described resilience.

Resilience Behaviours

- Can you tell me a bit about what behaviours you think might have an impact on resilience?
- What do you think improves your resilience and your ability to bounce back after a setback?
- What do you think might help sector leaders more generally in sustaining their resilience?

The initial consideration was that responses to each of these questions should be considered separately. On reflection, as the interviews were semi-structured and the stance was interpretive, these three questions naturally flowed into one another and continued the discussion on behaviours. Some responses were given specifically in response to questions 3 and 4, and these have been detailed under "personal" resilience and "general" resilience. Consideration was also given to the fact that answers were not given on actual behaviours per se but on perceived behaviours as identified by the interviewee.

The first reflection was that very few participants went into specifying separate positive and negative behaviours; indeed, some behaviours could be said to help or hinder resilience depending on the situation and how they were exhibited. As an example, adaptability could be seen as a positive response to dealing with change, while at the same time, increasing the risk of burnout if adaptation was relied on at the expense of control.

The second key reflection was that many of the behaviours given as examples could be identified as mindsets, defined "as a person's way of thinking and their opinions" (Cambridge University Press, 1995) or as a mental lens that selectively organises and encodes information. This leads to individuals having their own unique way of understanding an experience and thus their consequent actions and responses (Dweck & Yeager, 2019).

Finally, while discussing behaviours, some of the responses were classified as "factors", "a fact or situation that influences the result of something" (Cambridge University Press, 1995). These could be seen as external or environmental/contextual considerations, which may impact resilience. Responses falling into the categories of mindsets and factors are detailed separately.

Examples of behaviours that impacted resilience have been grouped into the themes, for example:

- Holistic
- Adaptability
- Communication
- Responsibility
- Acceptance of non-perfection
- Honest/Authentic
- Sharing/Peers/Teams
- Time/Control/Stability
- Research/Experience

There were a few outliers, such as:

- Celebrating success
- Decisive
- Persistence
- Consistent
- Writing

Holistic

The biggest area of responses regarding behaviours came under the theme of **Holistic**. The term holistic was chosen as it is characterised by the belief that the parts of something are intimately interconnected and can only be explained by referencing to the whole. It is a term that reflects the wider work-life balance aspects of responses.

Leaders discussed the importance of having a balance in life and the ability to switch off. Many highlighted that sometimes their best strategic thinking occurred in non-work time when running, gardening, or walking the dog. This observation closely linked resilience to behaviours associated with rest, relaxation, and recuperation, with a mention of quality or rest time as well as quantity. Some explained that activities, volunteering, and family time could be part of the rest and recuperation needed to be resilient at work. The importance of not working long hours or skipping holidays and making time for things and people outside of work was key.

Five sub-themes were identified within the holistic category:

- Non-work activities
- Work/Life balance
- Family/Friends

- Being human
- Volunteering/Faith/Humour/Mental well-being (outliers)

Many interviewees talked about **Non-work activities** – things they did outside of work that impacted their resilience. Being outside, walking the dog, exercising, gardening, and hobbies all featured. One response talked about the hour of gardening at the end of the day being the calm time they needed, with others explaining how they couldn't look at their phone while walking the dog or cycling. Being outside, exploring wild spaces, and walking by the sea were examples given. Balancing work and personal time, commonly described as **Work-life balance** (Ku, 2021; Guest, 2001; Fisher, 2010), featured highly. Many felt a sense of tension between their personal and professional lives and pressure to get the balance right.

With the period of research including time in lockdown, there was perhaps additional importance added to stepping away from the computer, getting outside, and finding time for the family when work could encroach into all areas. Some used examples of having set times when they stop looking at emails or days when notifications are switched.

Family and friends were discussed as being important to resilience: an outlet for emotions, a different space to step into, and an opportunity to have fun. Some detailed how they felt they could draw resilience from friends, family, and colleagues and how this helped them feel strong enough and confident that "they could do it". Others talked about how being a parent was important to their resilience.

Aspects of **Being Human** and staying "in touch" with one's personal emotions (Souba, 2011; Ladkin & Taylor, 2010; Smythe & Norton, 2007) often came into responses. One respondent felt that the words they most often thought of in terms of resilience were compassion and kindness. Another talked about bringing one's whole self to work and the need to "be human but show strength".

Not mentioned so often, but worth recording as relevant to some, were the outliers of **volunteering, faith, humour, and mental well-being**. One participant gave the example of volunteering as something that took them away from the day job and felt that doing something for others strengthened their resilience. There was a discussion around faith, how it helped them explore emotions in the workplace, and how it helped them bring "their whole self" to the role.

This holistic element was surprising as the question was about resilience behaviours in the context of participants' leadership roles, but many of the answers highlighted behaviours in life outside of work.

After holistic, **Acceptance of non-perfection** was the next most commented-on area and could be argued to show the pressure on leaders to "get things right first time" as opposed to trying things out with the possibility of failing and learning.

Being authentic, allowing oneself to be vulnerable, and fostering openness with teams and stakeholders came through strongly under the theme of **Honest and Authentic.** It was considered essential to be "true to yourself" and to be honest about your abilities. Finally, participants recognised the importance of being honest about needing to take breaks from work to preserve resilience.

Adaptability was mentioned as both a definition and a behaviour. Being able to respond positively to change, pressure, and stress was thought to be significant for resilience, as was the ability to adapt leadership styles as the situation demanded. The importance of good **Communication** at all levels, with stakeholders, funders, board, and staff, was mentioned often. Participants believed that often resilience was most stretched when communication failed or became challenging. One interviewee explained that good communication was even more valuable when resilience was low.

A range of behaviours were identified that related to **Peer Support, Sharing,** and consideration of **Teams.** There were comments on the importance of honesty and sharing with the board, about being open and reflective, and of having networks of peers both within specialisms and for external sources. Strong feelings of belonging were associated with having trusted peers, with terms like "gang" and "clan" or "tribe" reflecting the positive effects of having a place to share and learn and for peer support. Some talked about it as having a place where participants could "have a meltdown" and express negative emotions openly, enabling them to be calm and dependable and keep going in the leadership role. One participant mentioned that they could be the most resilient version of themselves if they could create resilience in their team too.

Another theme discussed was around **Control, Time, and Stability.** Participants felt that taking time to make decisions, staying calm, and ensuring some stability in a crisis contributed to resilience. Some leaders considered whether trying to be more controlling of the situation was a positive or negative behaviour. Some felt that they were more likely to be more controlling in difficult times, but there was a recognition that challenging situations often called for a more collegiate approach. The swan analogy was used again here, referring to appearing calm externally while struggling to keep stable underneath. Some talked about slowing down, listening, reading, and staying stable in difficult times and how that helped resilience both for them in their leadership and for their teams. One talked about resilient behaviour in challenging times as being "stabilising" and about how the focus was on finding areas that could be stabilised in times of crisis. The focus was not on jumping into solutions but on having a calm, reflective approach to the situation.

Responsibility often sits heavily on the shoulders of leaders, and the behaviour of recognising and sharing that responsibility was identified. Resilience was linked to an acceptance of the fact that not everything can be the direct responsibility of the leader. "Balancing" direct and delegated responsibilities was therefore seen as important to fostering resilience.

For some, the importance of doing their **Research,** gathering information, and taking their previous **Experiences** into account was a behaviour that impacted their resilience. Examples were given of crisis situations when it was helpful to look at what others had done and reflect on learnings that could be adapted to the current situation.

Celebrating success, being decisive, persistence, being consistent, and **writing** came through as outliers when mentioned in isolation but may be part of some of the previous behaviours detailed above. Celebrating success both as leaders and organisationally was felt to be a resilient behaviour, as was being decisive and being persistent in achieving one's aims. One interviewee discussed how writing things down helped, and others talked about putting a plan in place.

There were some responses which related more closely to the specific questions on general or personal resilience; these are detailed in the next section. Table 3.1 summarises the personal resilience behaviours found from the research before being discussed in more detail and evidenced through quotes.

Table 3.1 Holistic leadership resilience

Behaviours, mindsets, and factors which keep Third-Sector leaders resilient			
Coping dimension	Behaviour	Mindset	Factors
SHARING			
Has a willingness to support and learn from each other	Offers support Finds your tribe(s)	Open to sharing Open to listening	Gains support from a wide network Holistic: non-work
PROACTIVITY			
Considers well-being and actively puts support mechanisms in place	Seeks out support Understands what works for you	Reflects and learns Considers instinct and passion	Understands the wider environment Is aware of trigger points
BOUNDARY SETTING			
Is aware of the holistic nature of resilience	Ensures balance in all areas of life Asks for help	Balances Adaptability with stability Is honest about boundaries	Is aware of the changing world of work Engages governance and team

(Continued)

Table 3.1 (Continued)

Behaviours, mindsets, and factors which keep Third-Sector leaders resilient

WORKING SMARTER

Focuses on mission and impact	Accepts non-perfection Is authentic	Has confidence Plans ahead	Address issues Draws on information and experience

HOPE

Builds on passion and vision	Celebrates success Is persistent	Is optimistic Accepts positive feedback	Holds the vision Understands the context

RENEWING

Has a holistic approach to well-being	Acknowledges non-work activities Knows when to stop	Is self-aware Is honest about what you need	Understands what can be controlled Engages with team/family

Personal Resilience

The following themes emerged from the responses to the question, "What do you think improves your resilience and your ability to bounce back after a setback?"

• Moving forward	• Positionality
• Peers/Sharing	• Holistic
• Celebrate success	• Volunteering
• Making a difference	• Techniques
• Simplicity	• Acceptance of non-perfection
• Learning	• Knowing when to stop
• Planning/Authenticity/Integrity	

The ability to keep going or **moving forward** was highlighted as a behaviour under personal resilience. More than one response identified that it was not just about bouncing back, knowing when to "step forward"; to keep looking for opportunities to adapt to succeed.

The importance of **Peers** and **Sharing** with leaders both from within the sector as well as from other sectors were all seen as critical. Making sure **Successes** were recognised and celebrated was seen as particularly important for personal resilience. Knowing that doing what you do is **Making a Difference** was a motivator for some in relation to their personal resilience. Being "close to the front line" and seeing the difference being made helped leaders to continue their work and build their resilience. For some, the importance of **Keeping Things Simple** helped them to feel they could cope and sustain their resilience. All these aspects can be drawn from the quotes below.

Having **integrity** and "doing what you say you will do" were seen as fundamental to being **authentic** and building resilience. For some, the **position** they held made it feel harder to take risks as they were in the spotlight as the leader – and they had something to lose. This was seen by some as a drain on resilience. The **holistic** angle came through strongly for personal resilience. Having the head and the heart engaged made it easier to feel confident and build resilience. Aspects like volunteering and "a change of scenery" and non-work activities were again mentioned in this area.

Learning from experiences and considering what could have been done differently and what different approaches could have been taken was identified as a behaviour which could improve personal resilience. **Planning** and setting clear objectives helped to keep focus and strengthen resilience. Some mentioned specific **techniques** they used (coaching theory as an example) to help improve their personal resilience.

There was discussion around the **Acceptance of Non-perfection** which highlighted the importance of managing expectations (of self) and understanding that things won't always go as planned as detailed in this quote.

Finally, Knowing When to Stop was highlighted as specific to personal resilience. Continuing to push oneself beyond reasonable limits was seen as a drain on resilience.

General Resilience

The general resilience behaviours identified from the research include: Peers/Lonely

- Mentor support
- Confidence
- Leadership
- Non-perfection
- Factors
- Context
- Pressure

These themes were given as responses to the question, "What do you think might help sector leaders more generally in sustaining their resilience?" and will be discussed in more detail and evidenced through quotes.

For some, it was about having **Peers** and a supportive network. Not feeling **Alone** and knowing that others were having similar challenges was thought to be very helpful. Having an outlet in the form of a **Mentoring** relationship with someone outside of the organisation was found to help resilience. For some, it was about having the **Confidence** to be in the leadership role and to do what needed to be done. There was discussion about getting support in the **leadership** role rather than more generally in operations. For some, if that support was there, it led to feeling more resilient.

Being "good enough" was mentioned. Not overstretching rather than always trying to do everything and be the best was thought to be a factor in resilience. This had been mentioned previously under the theme of **Non-perfection.**

New Leaders

This section details the behaviours that were identified which would most help improve resilience in new leaders.

The next question asked was, "what advice leaders would you give to a those identified as new leaders, or what would you do differently with hindsight". This question was designed to try to pull out the key behaviours of resilience that were foremost in participants minds. When they looked back at their own experiences and thought about what would have been helpful to them as a new leader starting out, the behaviours which were thought to improve resilience in new leaders found from the research can be summarised as:

- Peer support network
- Cross-sector network
- Ask for help
- Selfcare
- Team
- Experience
- Positive feedback
- Not to please
- Reflect
- Non-perfection
- Role model
- Health
- Balance
- Clarity
- Learn from mistakes

The importance of having a **Peer Support Network** came out strongly in most interviewees' responses. Value was identified in having peers who understand the role and the sector with whom leaders can be honest about the challenges they face and discuss potential solutions. Some suggested that finding someone "further on in their career" would be helpful to share with, while others thought that a peer group of new leaders would be helpful. Some identified the need to have support, learning, and input from other **Cross-sector networks** to help them build resilience.

For others, value came from having a wider peer network from across sectors. Not being afraid of **Asking for Help** and admitting that things can be challenging was relevant. Feeling unable to ask for help was seen as a drain on resilience. Recognising one's limits and practicing **Self-care** to enable resilience in the role was identified as key. Having a good **Team** and a supportive "second in command" was suggested as something to focus on developing as a new leader.

Participants identified the importance of learning how to draw from **Experiences** from other walks of life, not just from a career perspective. It was thought that wider life experiences could give confidence and resilience, which could be drawn on in the leadership role. Hearing, noticing, and recognising **positive feedback** was something highlighted as being particularly relevant for those early in their leadership role.

Understanding that it is **not your role to please** and accepting the impossibility of pleasing all of the people all of the time was pertinent for early career leaders. Time to think and **reflect** on both the role of the leader and the strengths and weaknesses of the organisation was critical for those coming in new to the role. Not making quick judgements and presumptions but finding time to take stock even when there was pressure to make a quick impact was valued by respondents. Not having to strive for **perfection** all the time, being forgiving to oneself, and learning from mistakes were all identified as ways to build resilience for new leaders. The importance of taking risks which may lead to failures was also a factor here.

Thinking about who they may see as **role models** and what they could learn from their leadership styles and personas was given consideration for new leaders.

Keeping physically **healthy** when having the stress of being a new leader was identified as a particular focus for this group.

The importance of a work/life **balance**, of not letting work be all-encompassing and about having other things to help de-stress, were key elements of a new leader's resilience.

Getting **clarity** of what the role entails and what is expected and not "over promising and under delivering" in the early days as a new leader was highlighted.

The opportunity to make and learn from mistakes and not feel you must get things right first time came through for new leaders, as these quotes evidence.

Pulling It All Together

With the key findings pulled together, I was now at the stage of going back to consider the conceptual framework identified for further exploration from the literature review (shown in Chapter 2) and compare its relevance to the findings. The coping dimensions table shown previously was taken from Learning from Burnout, Developing Sustainable Leaders and avoiding Career Derailment (Casserley & Megginson, 2009) and was considered in relation to the findings of the research. I also considered if there is a reconceptualising of the framework which would be useful to sector leaders.

This original framework was based on "highflyers", a term defined as those in their 30s, ambitiously pursuing their career in a corporate context. To compare with the Third-Sector leaders, already at the top of their game and with a wide range of ages and years of experience, was a bit of a stretch.

The expectation was that in this different context, the coping dimensions to reduce burnout and thus be more resilient may be quite different.

The authors described burnout as "a work-related phenomenon most likely to affect those early in their career". The holistic findings detailed in the previous chapter would not then be expected to co-relate too closely to this framework. I decided to take each coping mechanism (and related behaviours) from the framework and compare it with the findings. The following observations were made.

The strong peer support and network findings mentioned under **sharing** closely relate to this coping dimension, and the mention of family and friends connects to the more holistic elements of support found in the study. There was occasional mention of what could be defined as "proactive resilience" under the **proactivity heading,** such as self-care and acceptance of non-perfection (new ways of doing things). The holistic nature of the behaviours could arguably be seen as a proactive approach. There was some mention of focussing on what was within control; this could be linked to an **Acceptance of non-perfection** and realising that not everything is within the leader's control.

The dimension of **Boundary setting** could not be co-related as strongly. Boundaries in the research findings were much more blurred in terms of what should be defined as "work time" and when it was starting to encroach into family or leisure time. This could be linked to the changing world of work previously described and the boundary between work and home being much less defined.

It could also be argued that the dismantling of silos between sectors and the breaking down of barriers to achieve societal change means that boundary setting in the way we work across external boundaries may be less defined. As an example, volunteering on a voluntary sector board could be perceived as work or leisure time.

Working smarter had both similarities and differences between the framework and the findings. There was talk of work and life intertwining and the importance of having a balance, but not the linear boundaries referred to in this framework. The findings on acceptance of non-perfection relate to the elements of not always getting it right. It links to the challenge in current times of the perceived risk of doing things differently and learning from mistakes.

Maybe surprisingly, **hope** did not feature as strongly in responses. This could be as it is seen as inherent in the Third Sector as opposed to the private sector, which the framework is based on. There was talk of optimistic mindsets, passion for the cause, and making a difference in people's lives, but the term hope was not evident. Seligman (2011) argued that the key to building resilience was optimism and that people who don't give up interpret setbacks as temporary, local, and changeable thus feel less helpless and more able to deal with the situation.

The link to **renewing** that exercise and sport help us with the ability to switch off from work does relate to the findings, and there was some consideration of how they also give time to reflect. Knowing when to stop, which was highlighted in the research findings, also relates to switching off. The difference in terms may be explained through the perception in the framework of life and work being more defined in the time when the coping dimensions research was initially carried out. The idea that leaders step out of one area to renew before stepping back into the other may explain the similarities which come from this area.

The expectation was that this framework would be very different from the findings of this research, but surprisingly, a significant number of similarities were identified. Despite differences in the date of study (13 years ago), geography, age, experience, and sector, the overarching difference is that the coping dimensions framework relates more to work and the organisation, whereas the findings from this research suggest that resilience is more holistic and the boundaries between work and life are not as defined. This could be due to changing times and how work is more flexible than traditional working hours or could be an element of sectoral-specific ways of working and thinking, as the original study was set in the private sector.

It may be worth considering the difference between coping mechanisms and resilience behaviours. Coping is defined as "the thoughts and behaviours mobilized to manage internal and external stressful situations and behaviours" and dimensions "an aspect or feature of a situation". Therefore, coping dimensions are ways in which highflyers cope in specific (work) situations. Behaviours are defined as "the way in which one acts or conducts oneself, especially towards others". The questions asked were specifically about resilience as a leader – but not in a work environment. This could indicate why the holistic element came so dominantly in response. Consideration could be given to whether previous studies asked questions about resilience and burnout specifically at work, and therefore the correlation between resilience at work and in wider life may not have come through as strongly. Herrman et al. (2011) found that definitions of resilience have evolved and referred to the evolution as positive adaptation, or the ability to maintain or regain mental health despite experiencing adversity. They consider the interaction of resilience with other areas of life, such as relationships and attachments. The fact that in this study, the behaviours mentioned were perceived behaviours from the leader's own perspective could also be an element for consideration.

In relation to the sector the highflyers were based in, the corporate sector, it could be argued that the Third Sector is not typical of business, so a difference in behaviour should be expected. The converse of this is that the Third Sector has "professionalised" over the years and leaders, and their organisations would not survive if they weren't led as effectively and efficiently as any private sector business. If we consider the public sector, Elliott (2020) suggests that public administration often operates in a crisis, making it very difficult to consider future design and delivery of services. It could be argued that the size and scale of most public sector bodies would mean that they have the ability to adapt and change. It could be argued that the size, scale, and background infrastructure of the public sector mean that those working in the sector are removed from the impact the sector can have and therefore aren't as likely to "take their whole selves" to the role.

A reconceptualising of the previous framework incorporates the findings from this research and is adapted to consider the behaviours, mindsets, and factors that may improve resilience for Third-Sector leader.

This reconceptualised framework shows the adapted coping dimensions found in the study relevant to Third-Sector leaders and shows them in a similar format to the previous framework. It then adds a column for mindsets and an additional one for factors. There is no "read across" in this framework other than of the headings of sharing, proactivity, boundary settings, working smarter, hope, and renewing, which are each shown under behaviour, mindsets, and factors. The mindsets and factors are relevant to that coping dimension but do not relate directly to that behaviour being shown.

The new framework shows the holistic areas which need to be incorporated for resilient, sustainable leaders in the Third Sector. It shows that under each coping dimension of sharing, proactivity, boundary setting, working smarter, hope, and renewing, as well as the coping dimension and behaviour, there is also a corresponding mindset and factor to take into account.

This reconceptualised framework interprets and brings together the findings from this research. It adds a contribution both to knowledge and practice and could lead to an adaptation of a range of tools with practical use.

Although this study comes from a qualitative axiology, the managerialist approach taken means that to have impact in practice, it may be helpful to show this more simplistically by using a "practitioner shorthand" of:

$$HLR = B + M + F$$

Where "HLR" is holistic leadership resilience, "B" is behaviour, "M" is mindsets, and "F" is factors. Thus, holistic resilience can be seen as an outcome of bringing together perceived behaviours with mindsets and factors. The coping dimension could be seen as the element of resilience and thus is not incorporated in the practitioner's shorthand. Although this may appear to be a formulaic representation, no numerical values are ascribed, and the representation is used as a practical tool to simply convey the ideas developed in this study.

The findings have shown that it's not just the things that you do – the behaviours – it's also how you do it – the mindset you have, and also the understanding of the environment you do it in that makes the difference in being a resilient leader.

Summary

This chapter has taken the reader through the key findings of the research and pulled them together into a reconceptualised framework as an adaptation from Casserley and Megginson to be relevant to Third-Sector leaders. It considered how the personal and professional elements of resilience come together and the interplay between our emotional resilience through looking after ourselves outside of work to make sure we don't burn out and the professional behaviours based on our values, integrity, and sense of purpose, which seems to be what allows leaders to continually adapt and feel resilient enough to continue.

The following chapters will go more in-depth into firstly the behaviours and secondly the mindsets and factors that are highlighted in Table 3.1.

Resilience Reflections/Analogy: The More You Know, the More You Realise You Don't Know

This phrase took on new meanings from both a personal and research perspective. I somehow expected a neat list of behaviours to flow from my questions – and struggled a bit with what to do with all the other aspects (which became mindsets and factors). It would have been easy to dismiss these as not what I was asking for, but they made sense and helped me understand how a whole life view on resilience had helped me get through difficult times.

References

Cambridge University Press. (1995). *Cambridge Dictionary*. https://dictionary.cambridge.org/

Casserley, T., & Megginson, D. (2008). Learning from Burnout. In *Learning From Burnout*. https://doi.org/10.4324/9780080942155

Dweck, C. S., & Yeager, D. S. (2019). Mindsets: A View From Two Eras. *Perspectives on Psychological Science*, 14(3), 481–496. https://doi.org/10.1177/1745691618804166

Elliott, I. C. (2020). The Implementation of a Strategic State in a Small Country Setting— The Case of the 'Scottish Approach.' *Public Money and Management*, 40(4), 285–293. https://doi.org/10.1080/09540962.2020.1714206

Fisher, C. D. (2010). Happiness at Work. *International Journal of Management Reviews*, 12(4), 384–412. https://doi.org/10.1111/j.1468-2370.2009.00270.x

Guest, D. E. (2002). Perspectives on the Study of Work-life Balance. *Social Science Information*, 41(2), 255–279. https://doi.org/10.1177/0539018402041002005

Herrman, H., Stewart, D. E., Diaz-Granados, N., Berger, E. L., Jackson, B., & Yuen, T. (2011). What Is Resilience? In *Canadian Journal of Psychiatry* (Vol. 56, Issue 5, pp. 258–265). Canadian Psychiatric Association. https://doi.org/10.1177/070674371105600504

Ku, L. (2021). Work-life Balance: What Really Makes Us Happy Might Surprise you. *The Conversation*. https://theconversation.com/work-life-balance-what-really-makes-us-happy-might-surprise-you-168446

Ladkin, D., & Taylor, S. S. (2010). Leadership as Art: Variations on a Theme. *Leadership*, 6(3), 235–241. https://doi.org/10.1177/1742715010368765

Reynolds, K. J. et al. (2010). Interactionism in Personality and Social Psychology: An Integrated Approach to Understanding the Mind and Behaviour. *European Journal of Personality*, 24, 458–482. https://doi.org/10.1002/per.782

Scamell, M. (2011). The Swan Effect in Midwifery Talk and Practice: A Tension between Normality and the Language of Risk Mandie Scamell. *Sociology of Health & Illness* , 33(7), 987–1001. https://doi.org/10.1111/j.1467-9566.2011.01366.x

Seligman, M. E. P. (2011). Building Resilience. *Harvard Business Review*, 89(4), 100–106.

Smythe, E., & Norton, A. (2007). Thinking as Leadership/Leadership as Thinking. *Leadership*, 3(1), 65–90. https://doi.org/10.1177/1742715007073067

Souba, W. (2011). Perspective: A New Model of Leadership Performance in Health Care. *Academic Medicine*, 86(10), 1241–1252. https://doi.org/10.1097/ACM.0B013E31822C0385

Chapter 4

Resilience Behaviours – *Juggling While Riding a Unicycle*

Introduction

This chapter will consider my own resilience behaviours during this time before exploring the behaviours found from the study in more detail. It will consider the findings in relation to the different questions asked. It will then consider how the findings relate to traditional styles of leadership.

My Own Behaviours

My studies are starting to impact life in many ways, and things maybe aren't so separate now. With my interviews finished, I find I'm getting involved in other aspects of academic life, including my first attendance at a research conference, "Voluntary Sector and Volunteering Research" as a "new researcher". The conference was the first opportunity to get together in person in a long period (since COVID). I had to submit an abstract to be accepted, write an academic paper, and present at the conference (new researchers' theme). I could almost hear my supervisors questioning why I was giving myself extra work (again), but the benefit and the experience well outweighed the challenge of finding the extra hours.

Learning from the conference included the understanding that peer support is very important to researchers too. There were similar challenges to mine being experienced by colleagues much more advanced in their research journey than I was. The feedback from my presentation was extremely helpful and supportive and made me feel that this maybe was a space I could be confident to inhibit. I met a few other early-career researchers from Scotland and suggested setting up a small group in Scotland to continue to meet.

The learning reminded me that I should "own it" more in this field and be a bit more confident. I started to feel like part of this peer network and realised that researchers are humans too, and maybe at last I was beginning to grasp the language. On reflection, I wonder if this would have

DOI: 10.4324/9781032627212-5

happened quicker if my studies hadn't coincided with the pandemic and that I had been more able to engage in person with peers along the way.

One relaxation of pressure came from stepping down from my Vice Chair role at the charity regulator after an eight-year term on the board, so one less task to find time for. I also started to think about my longer term planning and worked up some scenarios of how I might balance work, study, and leisure time going forward.

We were starting to come out of the pandemic, and it was a period of learning and reflection and maybe cautious optimism. I did reflect on how much the pandemic may have shaped my experience during the time of my studies. I'm sure it did in lots of ways, but it certainly made the topic of my research even more pertinent. At this stage, the realisation of how much work I still had to do was quite worrying, and I really had to keep a focus. I did feel some pressure to complete my studies in three years as the funding I'd managed to secure only covered this period, so it was a case of knuckling down and getting on with it.

Reflection also reminded me of the importance of chunking down, keeping going, and just taking a step at a time when things got tough. I also reflected on my role as CEO and how much I sometimes struggled with not liking rules or being told what to do – an occupational hazard when there are lots of rules around how research should be done and how much a framework had to be kept within.

I had also been diagnosed with osteoarthritis in my hips (not helped by sitting at a desk so much) and had to come to terms with the fact that I would have to have surgery at some point. I decide to take the "keep moving as much as possible" approach and sign up to a Zumba class! My other challenge is my parents and their increasing frailties and health issues. It sometimes feels a bit selfish to have so many things on the go that I have very little time to help and to spend with them. Continuing to stay active and to keep running are still outlets for me when the going gets tough.

I made the huge decision to make plans to leave my role after 18 years. After much reflection, I decided that if I got to 20 years, I would be "overstaying my welcome", so I should move on while I was ahead. It was a big step, and one that doing the doctorate was a large part of. It made me realise how much, as CEO, I was having to work at a surface level over so many areas and how sometimes it's good to have a narrower focus and go deeper. I also needed time over the summer ahead to focus on my write-up. Big changes ahead and a new chapter opening.

I still have moments of feeling overwhelmed. It turns out there is a lot of extra work involved in leaving my role. I had given six months' notice to plan a smooth exit (I hoped). I start to worry about not having an income and whether it's too early to retire. The time when I'd planned to finish up was fast approaching. There was a big relief in having time to study properly and get the thesis finished. As ever, I find I am worrying about practicalities about all the final "finessing", proofreading, checking references, layout, etc. rather than the most important bit, the content!

I then got COVID and had to cancel everything for ten days. This meant I had time to study and wrote the first draft of my learning journal (a compulsory – and marked – part of my doctorate) – and which has been the basis for the sections on my own resilience in this book. I also wrote my discussion chapter. It made me realise how much I could get done when I didn't have so many other things to do and had to stay home. This must be what it's like to be a full-time student! I'd been asked to speak on resilience and leadership at a few different sector events. I realised I had forgotten how much it helps to talk about what I am doing – something my supervisors had been advising in terms of reading out what I had written – but I realised that presenting it to others helped my thinking even more so. I have known for a long time that I "talk to think" rather than "think to talk" and realise that this is an extension of this mindset.

I had my mock viva, and feedback was positive. I was still working on my analysis, and using my questions as a framework for the analysis really helped. I was struggling at this stage to turn the data I had in the coding programme into something to write up in my findings. At a researchers' network meeting, I chatted with a colleague who told me she had used virtual whiteboards to visualise her thinking and findings. I decided to give it a try, and it was a game changer for me. I have always known I was very visual in how I think and learn, so this really worked for me.

The next period focused on writing up my findings and discussion chapters, putting everything together, working through each chapter to ensure continuity, and making sure I had done the best job I could. I reflected on the "acceptance of non-perfection" and how I would feel about something that was "good enough" and realised I really want something I can be proud of – but I knew there was a balance to be had of getting it done in the time I have and to the best of my ability within that time.

I evaluated where I had gotten to and concluded that I was where I wanted to be at this stage and could see a clear (ish) path for the final push ahead. I felt confident that any rocky road along the way could be navigated, and the challenges over the last few years had equipped me well to do this. I realise I now know what works for me, and in terms of writing, its… just write, go with the flow, then sense check, and finesse later.

Analysis of Behaviours

The questions asked in the study were focused on behaviours, which the Oxford dictionary describes as "the way in which one acts or conducts oneself, especially towards others". The study looks at behaviours as something that the leaders have some control over in terms of how they act in their roles, i.e., the act of leadership, while in the position of leadership. The questions specified behaviours, but because of the stance and approach taken, many answers are arguably of a wider nature and thus were categorised as mindsets or factors. This chapter will include a discussion around why it was decided to include all three in the findings to give a fuller picture of resilience as understood by sector leaders and thus the behaviours that may influence and improve resilience.

The table below shows the key findings from the four research questions focusing on resilience behaviours. When analysing responses, behaviours were coded from a general "resilience behaviours" perspective from question 2, but those that were more specific to questions 3, 4, and 5 were then pulled out and a separate section was added on each. When co-related in this way, it shows that the **holistic** theme was the most mentioned, with **sharing** and **peers** and **acceptance of non-perfection** being the themes that cut across all answers. For this reason, this chapter will first focus on these three aspects before discussing the wider findings (Table 4.1).

Table 4.1 Key findings

Resilience: Behaviours	Improves: Personal	Improves: Sector	New leaders
Holistic Non-work activities Work/life balance Family/friends Human Volunteering/faith/ humour/mental well-being (outliers)	Moving forward	Peers / lonely	Peer support network
	Peers/sharing	Mentor support	Cross-sector network
	Celebrating success	Confidence	Ask for help
	Making a difference	Leadership	Selfcare
	Simplicity	Non perfection	Team
	Learning	Factors	Experience
Acceptance of non-perfection	Planning/authenticity/ integrity	Context	Positive feedback
Honest/authentic	Positionality	Pressure	Not to please
Adaptability	Holistic		Reflect
Communication	Volunteering		Non-perfection
Sharing/peers/teams	Techniques		Role model
Time/control/stability	Non perfection		Health
Responsibility	Knowing when to stop		Balance
Research/experience			Clarity
Celebrating success/ decisive/ persistence/ consistent/writing			Learn from mistakes

Holistic Leadership Resilience

Holistic behaviours were those most strongly identified as behaviours that impacted resilience, but also as the behaviours that most impacted leaders' whole selves, both professionally and personally. This is a particularly interesting finding that did not feature strongly in the literature. My second question asked, "Can you tell me what behaviours you think might have an impact on resilience"? This question did not ask about "your" resilience specifically, or "your sector", but more generally as a way of moving from the first question, which focused on participants' understanding of resilience, to the second question, which brought the focus to behaviours. The definitions of holistic detailed below have been the basis of the use of this term in this study.

"Characterized by the belief that the parts of something are intimately interconnected and explicable only by reference to the whole" from a philosophical perspective, and from a "medical" perspective being "characterized by the treatment of the whole person, taking into account mental and social factors, rather than just the symptoms of a disease"

(Valentinuzzi, 2020).

This whole-person approach, incorporating all aspects of the leaders' lives, was the underpinning reason for this choice of term. Further definitions were also considered in coming to the decision to use the term holistic.

"Relating to or concerned with wholes or with complete systems rather than with the analysis of, treatment of, or dissection into parts holistic medicine attempts to treat both the mind and the body. Holistic ecology views humans and the environment as a single system".

(Merrian-Webster, 2022).

"A holistic approach means to provide support that looks at the whole person, not just their mental health needs. The support should also consider their physical, emotional, social, and spiritual wellbeing"

(NSW Health, 2020)

It is interesting that the term "holistic" was a definition used in relation to medicine which treated the whole person. The term "wellbeing" is often used in relation to the whole to describe staying well, having balance – and arguably, not burning out. This term was not chosen as a study of resilience focuses more on challenge and navigating these challenges rather than maintaining wellness.

It is very interesting that when asked what helps leaders at a sectoral level (as opposed to personally), the holistic aspects do not come through as strongly. It could be argued that when considering personal resilience, leaders do not recognise that their peers experience the same challenges. This linked to the often-mentioned sentiment that leadership is a "lonely place to be" and how valuable it is to have peer support. Respondents answered much more confidently on personal behaviours and less confidently on what they thought about the behaviour of other leaders in the sector.

Holistic behaviours highlighted in the responses did not only relate to work and were much more focused around how the leaders lived their lives. A picture emerged of leaders who saw their resilience as part of their wider way of being. Examples were given, such as the "beaker analogy", which implies that one's resilience as a leader can be impacted by stress or burnout in any area (beaker) of life and that solutions are most effective when considering the whole person. Others referred to this as a "reservoir of resilience", which should always be kept topped up.

The study specifically looked at resilience behaviours of leaders and not the overarching leadership styles, but it is worth considering the styles exemplified by Third-Sector leaders and the behaviours that are linked to those styles. The behaviours identified in this study could be seen to align most closely to the styles of Servant Leadership and Authentic Leadership.

Greenleaf's (1998) theory of Servant Leadership suggests that the servant-leader:

• Leads and serves with love
• Acts with humility
• Is altruistic
• Is visionary for the followers
• Is trusting
• Is serving
• Empowers followers

The understanding of resilience identified by Third-Sector leaders included values, trust, impact, and kindness, which could relate to serving and altruism. Being human and accepting non-perfection denotes humility and the importance of "making a difference". And the concept of "bringing whole self to work" and role modelling could be seen as visionary and empowering.

The four components of Authentic Leadership, according to George (2018), are:

• Self-awareness
• Relational transparency.

- Balanced processing
- Strong moral code

These components have been identified through the self-awareness theme of responses, through trust and values, and the importance of teams and peer support. Balanced processing could relate to the findings around balancing authenticity and maintaining a "game face", depending on the situation. This could be considered similar to the work of Vanderpol (2002), who found that many of the healthy survivors of concentration camps had what he called a "plastic shield". The strong moral code is evidenced through honesty and the importance of making a difference.

Bill George described the world that we live and work in as one of volatility, uncertainty, complexity, and ambiguity and proposed that the leadership response needed was one of vision, understanding, courage, and adaptability. The term VUCA was first used in 1987, from the work of Bennis, Warren G, Nanus, and Burt and their book, *Leaders: The Strategies for Taking Charge* (Bennis & Nanus, 1985). It could be argued that in today's complex world, these strategies are needed more than ever.

Another theme for consideration that came out of the research was around being authentic but adaptive. Participants felt that leaders need to reflect the many faceted aspects of themselves in their role. This wasn't seen as being unauthentic but instead was deemed necessary to adapt to changing situations. Importance was placed on not just what a leader does but also on why and how they do it. If the ethics, values, and culture they lead through are consistent, then the leader may exhibit flexibility whilst remaining authentic.

This holistic approach to leaders' resilience, seeing it as something that effects the whole person and every part of their life, means that we need to take a much more holistic view of how we approach improving resilience. We should not focus on resilience at work alone. Any intervention to improve resilience needs to take a whole-person approach too.

Before moving on from this section, the types of activities mentioned under the heading of holistic should be considered and discussed. When asked about resilience behaviours, a wide range of non-work activities were mentioned. These included gardening, football, walking, running, yoga, meditation, and much more. Often, these were the first answers given. The question was asked in a work setting, about participants role as a leader of a charity, but the answers related to things outside of work that made them more able to lead their organisation, more resilient, and less likely to burn out.

Work/life balance responses also came to the fore. If work was all-encompassing, then the opportunity to engage in activities outside of work that improved resilience was removed. There is a correlation here to the changing world of work, skills utilisation (Grant et al., 2014), and the move towards "work / life integration". The leaders interviewed were working mostly from home and would likely continue to do so to some extent, causing a blurring of boundaries, which yielded both positives and negatives. Work could now be adapted around lifestyle and family commitments but could also become all-encompassing and hard to get away from. Some described it as "not working from home; at home, trying to work, in a crisis".

Family and friends were often quoted as sources of resilience. Playing with the kids, out with friends, being listened to and sharing concerns with a spouse, or just being with people where you did not need to talk work. Being with those who knew you in a different guise and had different expectations all improved resilience. This could possibly be explained by the opportunity these aspects give to step outside the work environment, to be able to share in a safe space, and to be able to have fun.

The outliers of responses – volunteering, faith, humour, and mental well-being – gave an insight into holistic resilience. For some, volunteering and giving back boosted their spirits and gave them energy to face another day. For some, their faith was what kept them going. For others, it was "having a laugh" or focusing on their own mental well-being that helped them keep going, as humour and self-care were identified as positive resilience behaviours.

Acceptance of Non-perfection

Acceptance of non-perfection could relate to the pace of change over the period of study, and the increasing pace of change in today's world (Mitsakis, 2020). Leaders need to adapt and change, continually try new ways of working, develop new projects, and encourage more adaptive working with their teams. This change comes with increased risk and links back to Harari's (2018) assertion that we must "re-write our stories". If this means more risk of not getting it right the first time and experimenting with the new, then the acceptance of non-perfection is more important than ever before. It is also worth considering the complexity of the way the Third-Sector measures success. The purely financial measures traditional to the private sector are replaced by a "triple bottom line" of financial, social, and environmental factors. The quality-of-service delivery, impact of activity, and "distance travelled" are more relevant. Expectation of perfection, or of inflexible agreed results, from boards of governance, funders, and stakeholders could diminish resilience. This means that acceptance from these stakeholders (and from the leaders themselves) that they won't always get it right is seen as a critical aspect of resilient behaviours. The way projects are funded rarely supports research and development; thus, it is harder to take risks and try new things.

The public perception of charities and the increased regulation could have a part to play in Third-Sector leaders' resilience. Charities are held to high account to "do good" and to "make every pound count". It could be argued that they are held under more scrutiny than other sectors. Subsequently, any mistakes or errors make it even more difficult to accept non-perfection and the risk of failure through innovation and experimentation.

A perception that should be included in this chapter is that leaders are "not there to please". The possible prevalence of the Servant Leadership style in the sector, with common behaviours such as acting with humility and empowering others, means that there could be a paradox between the way we lead "to serve" and the need to make difficult, sometimes unpopular decisions.

Being human links to comments of being authentic, being vulnerable as a leader, and showing that it's okay to fail sometimes to eventually find the right answer. This must be balanced with what was termed "game face", when confidence must be shown as a leader to inspire and motivate others and appear in control. In current times with black swan type events with increased improbability and widespread ramifications (Taleb, 2007), many leaders had to have very heightened awareness of their environment and of their own behaviours and leadership styles to adapt accordingly.

The being human element manifested itself through discussions of building trusting relationships at all levels, both within and out of the organisation. Values, trust, and kindness came through strongly and could be linked to how these relationships are underpinned and developed. This all links back to the more holistic approach to resilience, as does the focus on self, which showed as a behaviour through understanding of resilience and was also identified as an element of mindset. Looking after oneself, being aware of possible signs of burnout, and knowing what keeps a leader well all have an impact on resilience.

Peer Support

Peer support, networks, and teams are all based on an understanding that resilience can be sourced from the people around you as a leader, both within the organisation or sector and from the wider worlds of life and business. The range of questions that this response came through and the number of types of peer support mentioned show an understanding that resilience is not only relevant to work but affects all parts of life.

Finding a peer support network (both within and across sectors), was seen as critically important to resilience. Almost all those interviewed referred in some way to it being "lonely at the top". Identifying a safe space to share and having peer support networks was critical to balance the loneliness. Interestingly, the networks mentioned weren't only of one type. Some participants mentioned internal teams (sometimes senior management teams), and there was a strong emphasis on networks of other Chief Officers in similar positions in the sector, but there was acknowledgement that it was good to share and learn from leaders in other sectors. There was the need to connect with others at a similar stage in their career, in a similar field, or in a geographical area. Finally, having a support network of family and friends out with work where the leadership aspect of the role could be "taken off" was critical.

Julien Stodd's (2017) thinking in his work on "Tribes, Communities and Society" suggests that the term "tribes" denotes social systems rather than formal systems and are strongly "trust-bonded" networks. He uses the term "cultural alignment", and in the way we are all part of complex social systems, it could be argued that in today's world we need a much larger number of "tribes" to be part of for each aspect of our lives. Although this study was not based around the COVID-19 pandemic, it could be argued that the notion of "having your tribe" around you became even more pertinent in a time when leaders were leading in isolation and apart from teams and families. The way of working during this study, where most were interacting online rather than in person, could have had an impact on responses. It could be argued that this change was not only of this time but that the shift to online working has sped up and is here to stay. Thus, the learning from the study, rather than being seen as of a specific time period, could be seen as future proofed and as a way to think going forward into an environment that is continually changing and at a pace that is increasing (Harari, 2018). Peer support was referred to in reference to building trusting relationships on a one-to-one basis. Mentoring, coaching, partners, friends, and having someone to "offload" to or use as a sounding board all had a positive impact on resilience.

This importance of "tribes" was considered particularly important for new leaders, which could be indicative of the fact that they are still building their networks and need the support when new while their confidence builds in the leadership role to a greater extent for those who have been in post for longer, are more experienced, and have support networks in place.

Summary

This chapter summarised the main behaviour findings, considered them in more detail, and explored their relationship to traditional leadership styles. It developed the idea that leadership resilience is more holistic than previously considered and that a whole-life look at resilience was the way forward. The next chapter will go on to look at mindsets and factors.

Resilience Reflections/Analogy: Juggling While Riding a Unicycle

This term was used by Professor John Mohan from the Third Sector Research Centre in his evidence to the House of Lords Select Committee (2017, p. 31), describing charity leadership as being not unlike "juggling on a unicycle".

The number of balls needed to be kept in the air while keeping the unicycle upright and moving in the right direction is a huge challenge which impacts resilience. We often find that if you drop one or two balls, it's the ones that are dropped that are noticed, not the fact that you still have the others in the air and the unicycle is still upright and moving forward. Not expecting perfection, knowing which are glass balls and will smash if dropped, and which are rubber and will bounce back is one of the key skills of resilient leadership. With all that in place, I've found that if you are juggling furiously, and suddenly two new balls from a different direction (or wider life) are thrown in, something is bound to drop off!

References

Bennis, W. G., & Nanus, B. (1985). *Strategies for Taking Charge*. Collins Business Essentials.

George, B. (2018). *VUCA 2. 0 : A Strategy For Steady Leadership In An Unsteady World*. 2–5. https://www.forbes.com/sites/hbsworkingknowledge/2017/02/17/vuca-2-0-a-strategy-for-steady-leadership-in-an-unsteady-world/#271a8a4013d8

Grant, K., Maxwell, G., & Ogden, S. (2014). Skills Utilisation in Scotland: Exploring the Views of Managers and Employees. *Employee Relations, 36*(5), 458–479. https://doi.org/10.1108/ER-09-2012-0069

Greenleaf, R. K. (1998). *The Power of Servant Leadership*. Berrett-Koehler Publishers.

Harari, Y. N. (2018). *21 Lessons for the 21st Century*. Penguin Random House.

House of Lords Select Committee. (2017). *HOUSE OF LORDS Select Committee on Charities Report of Session 2016-17 Stronger Charities for a Stronger Society*. https://www.parliament.uk/mps-lords-and-offices/standards-and-interests/register-of-lords-

Merrian-Webster. (2022). Holistic Definition & Meaning – Merriam-Webster. In *Merriam-Webster*. https://www.merriam-webster.com/dictionary/holistic

Mitsakis, F. V. (2020). Human Resource Development (HRD) Resilience: a New 'Success Element' of Organizational Resilience? *Human Resource Development International, 23*(3), 321–328. https://doi.org/10.1080/13678868.2019.1669385

NSW Health. (2020). *What is a Holistic Approach? – Principles for Effective Support*. https://www.health.nsw.gov.au/mentalhealth/psychosocial/principles/Pages/holistic.aspx

Stodd, J. (2017). *Tribes, Communities, and Society: a Reflection on Taxonomy | Julian Stodd's Learning Blog*. https://julianstodd.wordpress.com/2017/11/03/tribes-communities-and-society-a-reflection-on-taxonomy/

Taleb, N. N. (2007). *The Black Swan: The Impact of the Highly Improbable.* Random House Group. 1400063515

Valentinuzzi, M. (2020). Organismic Sets: What Are They? – EMBS. *IEEE Engineering in Medicine & Biology Society.* https://www.embs.org/pulse/articles/organismic-sets-what-are-they/

Vanderpol, M. (2002). Resilience: A Missing Link in Our Understanding of Survival. *Harvard Review of Psychiatry, 10*(2), 302–306. https://doi.org/10.1080/10673220216282

Chapter 5

Mindsets and Factors – *It's Not What You Do, It's the Way that You Do It*

Introduction

This chapter will take the reader through the latter part of my research journey and consider some of my own resilience challenges and supports throughout this time. It will then move the discussion on from behaviours to the mindsets and factors that were drawn from the research. It will look at why mindsets matter, that it's not just about the things that you do (behaviours), but also how you think that can make a difference. It will also consider what influences the environment, or factors, we work in play.

Personal Reflections

At this point in my research journey, I could just about see the light at the end of the tunnel – if only I could pull it all together and get my thesis finalised. I remembered a conversation with my supervisor, who, when discussing timelines, asked if I would panic if I was running behind. I realised that no, in the grand scheme of things, it's not something I would stress about. It's not a life-or-death matter for me. It's more around proving to myself I can do it, leading the way in the sector, my interest in peer support and the cohort model (a group of peers to act as study buddies), my interest in the subject matter, and the possible positive impact on the sector. It's also been about walking in others' shoes, opening new doors, and learning a new language (academic).

My main study buddy and I decided that taking ourselves away to my island home would be a good way to focus on this next stage and step away from the normal distractions. Although I now have a relatively comfortable place up there, we decided an old caravan nearby would be our study hub! We found we really enjoyed working and interacting in this way for our interactive study week. The rest of the cohort were online, and it felt a much nicer atmosphere than each working on our own.

DOI: 10.4324/9781032627212-6

If I think of my own mindsets during this time, my eternal optimism was helpful. I still hang on to just taking one step at a time and feeling confident that I will get where I need to be (physically and metaphorically). I also tried to hold on to a learning mindset but found that going from a role where I had lots of confidence and experience and was a big part of me – and almost second nature – to a new environment and context all together was very different. From always trying to expand on learning from a place of knowledge and experience, to almost starting with a blank page (on the processes, environment, and culture of academia – but not the content of the study) takes much more consideration and energy, something I hadn't really reckoned on. Self-belief maybe came into it to. Being at a stage in life where I knew I had survived through tough times gave me the strength to keep going.

I've talked a lot about the environmental factors during this time, but the other factors which impacted me were the importance of a strong relationship with the board and a shared belief in what we do. Finally, exhaustion was definitely a factor I had to contend with. From the juggling act of work, study, and family to the mental exhaustion of loss, continued challenges of the pandemic, and increased workload from all of the above, I had to often go back to focusing on myself, time for me, and doing whatever I needed to do to keep me going (from a long bath to digging the garden to lying in a hammock or going for a run)!

As mentioned in Chapter 4, in my last year of studies, I had decided to leave my CEO role to focus on the final push to pull my thesis together and submit it before the end of the academic year. It was a big step, which I thought I had planned well, giving six months' notice for an orderly recruitment and handover, but a range of challenges meant it didn't quite go to plan and an interim CEO had to be put in place. I wanted to leave well and worried about "my baby" (ACOSVO), whom I had seen through from being a toddler to a stroppy teenager to a young adult I could be proud of. After finishing up, I had a few months over the summer working on the thesis write-up, but with a nagging worry about my decision to manage without a job – or a salary – and whether I had "jumped too soon".

While having this thought, I was contacted by a recruiter about a role I thought would be a fascinating direction for me – not part of the plan at all. I had planned to finish my current job, spend the summer on my thesis, and then take a break before developing a portfolio career the following year. My argument on why I wanted the job was that through my studies, I had enjoyed the deeper focus on leadership rather than being CEO and leading an organisation. It feels a fitting "end" (and new beginning) to my journey over the last three years. I had thought I might go more into the academic world, and I don't want to lose this thinking completely, but as the role involves staying abreast of emerging leadership theories, this may be a way to combine both to help bring worlds together and join some interesting dots.

The role involved working in the public sector, connecting a wider sphere of organisations across sectors with a focus on leadership. I was offered the job with an agreed to start date of October, after I had submitted my thesis. Very quickly I was approached to start earlier and agreed a part-time phased start. I should have realised that taking on a challenging new role in a new sector when I was trying to finalise a three year research project (which I had planned to take time out to do), wasn't good for my own resilience, especially as I was becoming more aware of needing to be around to support my parents, and my own arthritic hips weren't very happy with the amount of time spent at a desk. Although COVID times were almost behind us, most of the work was still online, and most staff weren't keen to go fully back to offices, with some having been recruited from across the country!

Another example of how this next section on mindsets and factors has a part to play in resilience. My learning (or growth) mindset got excited about a whole new direction, and there was probably an "ego" element of how I saw myself if not as the leader I had been for a considerable time. Many factors had a part to play too. From the challenging environment of funding in the charity sector, of being exhausted and needing a change, to even the financial environment more widely and not earning a salary, along with the uncertainty of the growing conflict in the world and the need for security. They all had a part to play in my decision – and my resilience.

This next section will now consider the final stages of the research and the important, unexpected findings that the responses to the research questions on resilience behaviours brought a wider consideration and thus understanding of resilience.

Mindsets and Factors

Although the study aimed to consider resilience behaviours, it concluded that behaviours cannot be considered in isolation and that mindsets and factors must also be taken into account. This section will go into more detail on how this decision was made and give an overview of the findings.

Mindsets

Mindsets are defined as "the established set of attitudes held by someone" (Oxford Dictionary, 2022) and have been used to categorise the responses to the questions on behaviours which could be defined as "attitudes" or

Table 5.1 Mindsets

Mindsets (Behaviours)	Mindsets (Understanding)
Self – Self-aware	Self-care
Self-belief	Knowing yourself
Self-reflection	Positive feedback
Learning	Negative
Confidence	Calm
Honesty	Integrity
Individual/Team/Organisation	Morale
Optimistic	Openness
Passion	Purpose
Planning	Stability

ways of thinking and being. The decision to define these themes as mindsets rather than behaviours was a difficult one. The fact that these themes could be seen as something that you are rather than something that you do was the deciding element, even though they were responses to questions on behaviour. It could be considered that respondents thought that they behaved in a particular way because of who they are and how they think.

It may be considered that the themes identified were indicative of leaders having a growth mindset and its link to resilience. Dweck and Yeager (2019) argue that in a growth mindset, people believe that their most basic abilities can be developed through dedication and hard work. They assert that brains and talent are just the starting point to success and that this growth mindset leads to a love of learning and a resilience that is essential for achieving success.

This next section details the answers, which were thought of as mindsets rather than behaviours, meaning they relate to the way we think, rather than the way we behave. The responses detailing mindsets were unexpected as the questions were asked about perceived resilience behaviours. The mindsets found from the research can be summarised in this Table 5.1 and will then each be considered in more detail.

Selfcare

The most mentioned theme of **self** was further broken down into six sections: self-aware, self-belief, self-reflection, self-care, knowing yourself, and positive feedback. **Self-aware** or being aware of one's own abilities and your own limitations was thought to be vital to resilience. **Self-belief** was defined as knowing that you are doing the right thing as a leader and believing in yourself to keep going. **Self-reflection** was defined as being able to ask yourself the right questions – to reflect on the situation, how it arose, and what can be learnt from it. **Self-care** was identified as a key part of developing a resilient mindset – proactively identifying and addressing mental or physical health issues, rather than waiting until things needed fixing. **Know yourself,** linked to being self-aware, was defined as knowing what works for you and what doesn't in terms of your resilience. **Positive feedback** was defined as getting feedback that, as a leader, you are doing a good job. This was thought to help build resilience.

The term "selfcare" has been used as an overarching theme for self-aware, self-belief, self-reflection, self-care, knowing yourself, and positive feedback. This theme was considered under the wider heading of "mindsets". It links back to the personal rather than the organisational view of resilient leadership and how the way leaders look after themselves is as important to their resilience as the behaviours they exhibit in carrying out their roles. Bagi (2013) suggested that burnout could be reduced, and thus leaders may be more resilient if they developed a greater sense of self-awareness and a healthy identity, developed greater emotional resilience, and practised self-care.

Being aware of one's own resilience and what improves personal resilience rather than a more "blanket" solution was key. This links back to the importance of "being human" and recognising the human aspects of leadership. Having self-belief and confidence as a leader was valuable. To feel strong and confident enough to make decisions at a leadership level and inspire that confidence in others built a feeling of resilience and a belief that solutions could be found. Self-reflection was part of the learning journey, considering what had gone well or not so well and what could be learnt from that built resilience. Self-care was an area that featured high on the list for new leaders. This could be indicative of their level of confidence in bringing in experience from other parts of their lives to remind them how to bounce back from challenging times. It could be part of "knowing yourself", as they may not be as familiar themselves as a leader in the early days of the role – thus less able to identify how to look after themselves at a time when self-care is crucially important. Another area to cover for new leaders is how they are encouraged to think about their own resilience. Grant et al. (2014) discuss skills development in career progression to leadership roles, but resilience building is not featured as one of these skills.

This exploration of self links back to the work on cultural intelligence and emotional intelligence. Being self-aware enough to adapt to both emotional and relational issues while assessing the cultural implications of the environment being operated in connects with the "whole self" approach mentioned by respondents.

Leaders talked about bringing their whole selves to the role, and this meant that when they were "running on empty", it impacted all aspects of their lives, and thus their resilience was further impacted. This could be linked to the co-relation with compassion fatigue and how much leaders in the sector care about what they do. It could also be linked to servant and authentic leadership styles, as previously discussed.

The mindsets also identified humility, instinct, responsibility, and listening as outliers.

Curiosity, **learning,** and understanding all came into the responses. Treating every experience as an opportunity to learn was seen as a way to be more resilient in the leadership role. Examples were given of difficult experiences that, when seen as learning experiences, could be less negatively impactful.

Linked to self-belief, respondents talked about how having **confidence** in themselves and in their positions positively impacted resilience. Being **honest** about the difficulties of leadership and "role modelling that sometimes it is okay to not be okay" was seen as significant.

Respondents felt that when connected to their **teams** and **colleagues** and when there was trust between them, their resilience was higher. This led back to previous comments about not everything being the leader's responsibility and that a supportive team and **organisation** helped build resilience. Considering the **morale** of the team and the organisation, the motivation behind it, and the leaders' role in that was a factor in resilience.

The importance of having an **optimistic** mindset was thought to have an impact on resilience. It was felt that this stopped the negative spiral of self-doubt and negative expectations that could dent resilience. Leaders talked about being their own worst critic and how this could be a **negative** mindset to have.

Leaders talked about their **passion** for the cause and for the sector and how that helps them to "go the extra mile". Being values-driven and having **integrity** both internally and externally was thought to aid resilience. Having a clear **purpose** and aligning to that purpose was significant, as was being able to articulate that purpose to others.

Being **open** when times are difficult – both for the leader, the team, and the organisation – and open to learning from situations was thought to be a mindset which aided resilience.

Having a **plan** in place and having thought through contingency plans helped to build resilience. Again, the swan (or duck) analogy was mentioned as an example of how the ability to be **calm** in a crisis helped to build a resilient mindset. "Remembering to breathe" when stressed was a pertinent point. **Stability** came through as a mindset as well as a behaviour when it was discussed in terms of how stability of governance, of funding, and of a team could impact resilience.

Outliers of **humility, instinct, responsibility,** and **listening** were worth mentioning as significant to a few leaders interviewed. Humility was seen by one to be "vital" in that any success is shared and they are only as good as the team around them. For another, going with gut instinct was key, and for another, the importance of listening to others and really hearing what they are saying and how they are feeling.

Factors

The final term of classification used was "factor", defined as *"a circumstance, fact, or influence that contributes to a result"* (Oxford Dictionary). It could be argued that the questions were about behaviours – begging the question of why factors were included. The reasoning is that these factors were identified as having an impact on behaviours. Therefore, both concepts have a part to play in the exploration and thus understanding of "resilience behaviours in Third Sector leadership". This shows that although leaders identified in a very personal way with their own resilience, they were also aware of things around them that could have an impact on their resilience.

The responses that were identified as factors which impacted behaviours are shown in Table 5.2. The first column were answers given when asked what behaviours impacted resilience, and the second column were answers given to the question on understanding resilience.

The most mentioned factor was **governance** and the importance of having a supportive board. Some mentioned how helpful the board had been to support them through difficult times and how crucial it is to have good communication and be direct and honest with their board. If the leader is not supported by their board and the relationship is not strong, this can negatively impact resilience.

The **context** of the situation was often brought up by participants when asked about behaviours. The funding situation, the political landscape, the area of work, how partners were working together, what the regulatory situation was, and how the mission and purpose sat with the context of that time all needed to be considered. Identifying early **trigger points** which impacted resilience was a frequently considered issue. It was vital

Table 5.2 Factors

Factors (Behaviours)	Factors (Understanding)
Governance	Information/Experience
Context	Control/stabilising/addressing issues focus
Trigger points	Bounce back
Exhaustion	
Team	
Writing/planning/time as leader/ motivation (outliers)	

to recognise when resilience was being stretched and what may be causing strain. If identified early, this could mitigate further pressure.

Exhaustion was mentioned as being a factor, alongside how it impacted on what behaviours were exhibited. Examples were given of times when leaders felt compelled to continue working even when "the tanks are empty" and how difficult resilience could be in times of exhaustion. Dealing with challenges continuously while exhausted was when leaders felt most vulnerable. This links back to a previous point about knowing when to stop, taking time to rest and reflect, and the importance of self-care.

Although the impact of working with a **team** is considered in the behaviours section, there were occasions when it was mentioned as a factor which impacted the behaviours exhibited.

A few outliers that were mentioned as additional factors that impacted resilience were **time as leader** and **motivation** from the team around them.

To give some perspective, if the wider context and factors of the sector are considered at this point (ACOSVO, 2021) carried out a well-being, diversity, and succession study and found that:

Scotland's sector leaders showed a huge disparity in feelings of well-being within work and outside of it. Around 86% rated their well-being outside of work as "good" or "excellent", but this dropped by a third to 52% when in relation to work. Around 43% described their work well-being as "poor", whereas only 14% gave this rating outside of work.

Around 39% of leaders highlighted that they had felt the need to take time off for stress and burnout within the last year but didn't feel able to do so, with an additional 13% taking the time off.

Many leaders receive little support in their role other than "regular contact with their board" (69%) and an "annual appraisal" (52%). Professional support networks like ACOSVO and having a mentor were highlighted by 54% and 33% of respondents as a source of support, with "time" selected by 43% as being the biggest hurdle to getting the support they need.

More than half of respondents (53%) said they wanted to leave their role in the next five years, with 71% of this group looking to leave in less than 2.

This showed that well-being at work and the context the leader is working in impacts resilience, and if looked at holistically, it may be impacting life outside of work too. Thus, making leaders more likely to burn out and have reduced resilience. This aligns back to the holistic approach to leadership resilience and how taking our whole lives into account and thinking about how we balance resilience across this wider perspective means the things we do to build resilience outside of work can balance our resilience at work.

The End of the Research Journey

With the research and write-up now complete, it was time to submit my thesis. I lost count of how many times I checked and double checked I was submitting the final version, and my finger did hover over the "send" button for quite some time, but then it was done! Three years of hard work and juggling were complete – almost. I still had to sit my Viva (Viva Voce), where I would have to defend my thesis in front of an examination panel.

The day did come, and after being a bit nervous at the start, I actually quite enjoyed a chance to argue my stance and talk about my work. I had spent quite a bit of time preparing, as it was a few months after submitting. As tempting as it had been to put it all aside for a while and take a bit of a break, I knew I had to keep it fresh in my mind and be ready to be questioned.

For those interested in the format, after questioning by the panel, you wait outside while they convene, to then be brought back in to hear the result. It's a pretty anxious wait! I was brought back in to be told I had passed with minor amendments (only about 5% pass with no amendments, so this was a great result. Major amendments would have meant a much more comprehensive rewrite). I wanted to run outside and whoop – and call friends and family to let them know – but then found out it was traditional to then have refreshments and a more informal chat and be seen as a peer with your academic colleagues. As wonderful as that was, I felt I had to stay professional while full of excitement – not an easy task!

To conclude this research part of this book, the final stage was my graduation (after making my minor amendments and resubmitting within an approved timeline – and having them accepted). This was a grand affair with family in attendance, rounded off a few days later with a wider family BBQ – where I announced I was about to write a book!

Summary

This chapter has considered why mindsets and factors must sit alongside behaviours when considering what keeps Third-Sector leaders resilient. This whole life look at leadership resilience is underpinned by this thinking. This is the final chapter relating to the research part of the book. Part two will move to what this means for us as leaders and how we use the findings to consider new ways of working. First, we must consider the changing world of work in the next chapter.

Resilience Reflections & Analogy: It's Not What You Do, It's the Way that You Do It

To go back to the findings in this chapter, the often-used phrase that people don't remember what you do, but how you make them feel, is very relevant. If you think of how an optimist and a pessimist might carry out the same behaviour, but in very different ways, it might help consider why mindsets really do matter. Also consider carrying out the same behaviour in two very different environments – one hostile and one supportive. Both examples show that behaviours alone don't underpin resilience without considering the way you think as a leader and the environment you operate within. I'm hoping that by sharing some of my own experiences throughout this journey, I can demonstrate how all parts of my life impacted both my studies and my leadership role.

Reference

ACOSVO. (2021). *Wellbeing, Succession & Diversity in Scotland's Voluntary Sector Leadership*. ACOSVO. https://acosvo.org.uk/resources/wellbeing-succession

Part 2

The Way Forward

The Changing World of Work – *Change Has Never Been So Fast but Will Never Be So Slow Again*

Introduction

Before moving to the implications for leadership resilience that can be drawn from the research, it is important to consider the changing world of work and life. Many of the traditional leadership theories I explored in my studies were set in earlier times. The way we work now, anywhere, at any time, on any device is a huge shift from working 9 to 5 in an office with strict rules and regulations on how we should work. The expectations from the emerging workforce will also be considered. This chapter will explore these changes and what they mean for our holistic leadership resilience.

My Own Journey

My new job was ramping up, and I was starting to understand some of the challenges and constraints of public sector systems and governance – and beginning to appreciate the freedom I had in my previous role and sector. This really brought home to me the importance of programmes such as leadership exchange and the concept of cultural intelligence – both discussed in later chapters. It also helped me start to consider whether what I had learnt about resilience in one sector could be adapted and implemented in another. It brought to the fore our misconceptions and differences in cultures and language between sectors and helped reinforce the importance of the concepts I had been developing for learning and understanding between sectors.

I had an amazing team in my new role, all trying to make a difference in an area with lots of challenges – but I struggled a bit with the balance of supporting them in my leadership role, building a new team, and at the same time, still learning the complexities of the new environment I had moved into. Alongside all of this, as always, change was constant!

DOI: 10.4324/9781032627212-8

To go back in time and explore a bit of my own journey adapting to the speed of change, I've had a few personal challenges drive it home to me. From increasingly having to ask my grown-up kids for help with technology, when I have always prided myself on being able to keep up – to feeling my age when volunteering to conduct mock interviews with young people about to leave education. I've also seen how disabling it is to older people (e.g., my mother) who can't use the internet and no longer have the option of using high street banks to pay bills or look after their money.

When I look back at when I started working in a bank in the late 1970s, women weren't allowed to wear trousers. We had to give up work when we got married, and I wasn't able to sit any banking exams – even though I asked several times. I was always put off and didn't know any other woman who had passed them. I was once temporarily promoted to "head teller" when the previous one retired, until they found an older male to fill the role.

We stamped paper cheques, counted paper money, used calculators, had a pool of typists, kept banks of files, had a safe like you see in the movies, and had an archive of paper. There were banks on every street corner, and the only way to pay in or take out money was to go to a bank. Security men with helmets and visors picked up and delivered cash, and shopkeepers brought in bags of money at the end of the day (my pet hate was the bloody notes from the butchers that smelt awful).

I'm not even state retirement age and don't feel that old, but this is an indication of how much the world has changed in just over 50 years. In some ways it doesn't seem a long time ago, but in others it seems like another world.

To reflect on behaviours, mindsets, and factors during this time and in my new role, I realised I was behaving in a way that I knew worked for me when leading a team in one environment and had to stop and think if it would still work so well in a different one. I quickly realised that my values around how I led were something I had to hold on to, and as long as I could hold on to this core element, then how I had to adapt to changing systems could be more flexible. I had prided myself on a learning mindset and eternal optimism, but both were challenged to some extent. I had been learning through my studies, but in some ways, being in a different role (i.e., being a student, not a leader) meant that the adjustment was easier than trying to be the type of leader I wanted to be in an unfamiliar world. My optimism waned in light of the complexity of the systems and the amount of time that bigger systems need to change. Some of the things I had stressed about before (how we had to turn on a pin and continually adapt and change to meet changing needs) suddenly seemed like they were easy wins now compared to the challenges of changing quickly in a larger system – think juggernaut – small car scenario. The environment, or factors, had the biggest shift – both in terms of my familiarity and in terms of the difference and the need for continual change at scale.

As ever, I found my own resilience strengthened by both my new connections and my long-standing support network. It reminded me of the importance of having a balance of peer support (or tribes) across different spheres of life and work. My running buddies helped encourage me out when I could have spent every hour at my desk, my new colleagues supported me through learning this new language, and my Third-Sector network helped me stay grounded by reminding me of the wealth of knowledge I held, which was still so useful.

My island home was also an escape, and a reminder that this new world had the advantages of being able to work from anywhere. We had recruited from a much wider geography in my new role, so the expectations of getting together were very different. This meant I did find it more of a challenge to build those more holistic and human bonds online, and we all tried to make sure that we did still get together in person where possible – and took turns to facilitate so we could learn from each other. It definitely felt like walking the talk in terms of experiencing a very different context and way of working.

This next section will consider the speed of change in the workplace, the expectations of the future workforce, and how to ensure that we don't lose sight of holistic leadership resilience through these changes. Change has come across all aspects of work and life – how we think, how we work, how we play, how we see the world – and how our resilience is impacted.

Speed of Change

To reflect on the context of the future of work discussed in the introduction to this chapter, the speed of change in how we live our lives and the part work must play could all have implications in relation to the findings of my research. This section will consider these changes and then move to the implications on the emerging workforce, our future leaders, but will also look through the perspective of those leading now who have understood the role of the leader from a very different perspective over their years of experience and now must adapt to those changes.

Recent studies have shown that there are some challenges between the expectations of work from young people and the employers' (or leaders) readiness for the young workforce. It can be a difficult balance. Add to the equation the ageing workforce as pension age increases, and people live longer and work for longer, which means that both extremes of these expectations are at play at the same time. The plus side is that we stay healthy longer, but the challenges to workplaces of being suitable for such a wide spectrum of ages and expectations of their workforce and meeting the expectations of both can be a difficult juggling act.

This chapter comes with the understanding that I'm making huge generalisations in some cases, and I am also aware that I am seeing things through the perspective of an almost pension-age woman.

But it does make it interesting to consider from the perspective of what resilience means across the age groups. This is not something that I have studied specifically, but this chapter looks to align what I have experienced as a leader with a wide-ranging workforce, reading from others who do look at this specifically, and also learning from wider life and family.

The table below is an example of some of the changes that we have seen over recent years. It is given as an example of how the employee has evolved in how they must think and work. If we think of the leader from both an employee perspective and as a leader of those employees, we can see how our working life has changed and how it could be argued that life and work have become more closely entwined. Therefore, it may be less surprising than initially thought that resilience is seen as much more holistic across life and work (Table 6.1).

The influence of this thinking on the leader means that they must lead in a different way to incorporate the employee's more holistic approach to work and life, but they must also consider what this means to them for their own resilience and how they sustain it. Their resilience could be further strained by the "always on" expectation and thus the lack of time and space to access the holistic activities that their resilience relies upon.

I remember being told that we were doing our future leaders a disservice when, as CEOs, we would go on holiday and say, "I'll keep an eye on my phone / email in case of emergencies". In the past, we learnt to be

Table 6.1 How work has changed

Past	Current / Future
Work 9–5	Work anytime
Office based	Work anywhere
Company equipment	Use any device
Clear progression routes	Create your own progression plan
Clear work expectations	Focus on outcomes in your own way
Information gathered/stored	Information shared/open
Human-centric data	Generative AI
Clear hierarchy	Shared leadership, collaborative working
Email communication	Multiple communication methods
Learning plans	Ongoing learning and adapting
Formal supervision	Supportive feedback
Low number of roles and sectors experienced	Increasing number of roles, companies, specialisms, and sectors experienced

leaders by stepping up to the plate, dealing with the unexpected, and having to make decisions in cases when "the boss" wasn't around. How much harder are we making it for them to grow and learn if we are always there to step in when the going gets tough? – and how does this way of thinking impact our own resilience if we never really take a break?

I also remember holding a conference in 2014 entitled "Keeping Ahead of the Game", where we considered the huge amount of change that we were having to keep up with. Looking back now at the time of writing in 2024, we can see that in 2016 alone, we created more information than we had in the last 5,000 years collectively!! From a quick online search, it's easy to see examples of the change that is going on around us:

- The older generation is living longer, and the "new" generation is dying younger.
- We work for longer but often start working at an older age (study, gap years, etc.).
- Jobs have had a huge shift from "a job for life" to a zig-zag progression and a closer alignment to values and interests where possible – and the development of the "gig economy", where we can work at times that suit us – or when there is a need.
- Leisure often includes scrolling, gaming, and losing ourselves in social media – all in our own homes while being sedentary.
- Diseases of old age are affecting people younger (hypertension, high cholesterol, diabetes, etc.).
- The way we access data has changed. We expect instant answers immediately with a wide range of sources – some more credible than others.
- Communication with work, leisure, and family can all be the same devices.
- Algorithms mean we often have our own biases confirmed by only seeing online content based on what our interests are deemed to be.

I've even recently had an airport lunch brought to me by robot! Throw in AI, climate change, and world conflicts, and no wonder our resilience is challenged. It's an interesting consideration when we think of times when we didn't have access to all this knowledge, were there positives as well as negatives? I know sometimes I have to switch off the news and consider "pulling up the drawbridge" and living the remote island life for my own resilience.

Generational Changes

I've heard that the jobs we are currently educating young people for won't exist by the time they leave university, but I've also heard that when asked what they want to do with their lives, many young people say they want to make a difference in the world – but often aren't sure how best to do this.

In terms of expectation of work (Grant et al., 2021), and more recent studies by the same author have shown that young people describe themselves as hard-working, enthusiastic, creative, and trustworthy and envisage a workplace that provides exciting, varied, and challenging work. They feel they communicate well and work effectively as part of a team. They think the ideal workplace should be "fun, creative, lively, relaxed and flexible". They feel they are good with technology, but there has also been the assertion that this may mostly be with social media and applications rather than work-based technology.

The flexible working that has increased through COVID has led to an expectation of flexible hours and working from home options. Young people hope to "work to live", not "live to work", and that work should be flexible around their wider interests. They expect managers to get to know them as a person and offer support for that whole person rather than just work performance. They are keen to have good pay and conditions and job security but would not stay in a job that was to the detriment of their mental health – or if they don't enjoy it or feel it aligns with their values. Although job security is important, there is not the expectation of a "job for life" in the way that past generations had.

The openness to consider well-being, resilience, and mental health has been seen as a positive, but it could also be argued that older leaders or managers may not feel equipped to lead and support in this way. It was also found in the research that younger workers need clear induction, which also covers the softer expectations of an employee, the unwritten rules on behaviour, dress, social media use, etc. There was also perceived to be a better understanding of the role the workplace had to play in ensuring fairness, diversity, and difference, and the younger workforce had an expectation that their rights and well-being would be protected and understood by staff of all ages.

Resilience was seen as a particular challenge for young people. Even if they seemed assured outwardly, it is recognised that they develop confidence alongside life and work experience, and there may be fewer opportunities for this, especially when considering softer skills. The impact of the pandemic and remote working means that in-person social interaction is experienced to a lesser extent.

When my career began, you would never think of going to your boss to say you were stressed and needed their support, and for the organisation to take your needs into account, you were expected to do your job and not let the organisation down no matter what was happening in your life or how you were feeling. You were disciplined if you didn't behave or even dress in the right way. I'm not saying the changes aren't right, and we shouldn't be supported at work; I'm just saying that as a leader, it's a whole new world in how we lead, and if you go back to read some of the classics of leadership books, it could be hard to translate to today's working environment.

In my own experience as a leader, I've not only seen some positive moves but also some that can contribute to challenges in how we lead. Staff have more rights, and we are more aware of their wider support needs. Employers rightly have to try to meet those needs, but leaders can feel stuck between being able to meet the needs of their beneficiaries/clients/customers at the same time as their staff. What do you do when you have three staff all needing time off for stress or family challenges, the same week that you are running much-needed support groups for disadvantaged and vulnerable individuals in need – or have a contract to fulfil by a deadline?

Mentoring and reverse mentoring can be useful to develop an intergenerational workforce. I've had my own experiences of this, from having a mentor to support me through different stages of my career, to feeling the benefit of reverse mentoring as an experienced leader. This involved being matched with a young person at the start of their career who has leadership aspirations. To say I learnt as much from the young person as they did for me is probably an understatement. To gain an understanding of their world and to see my world through their eyes really made me think carefully about my own perspectives (and misconceptions) and to reconsider how I lead my younger workforce.

Third-Sector Workforce

To take this discussion from a Third-Sector perspective, awareness of the sector as a potential career option has been quite low in my discussions with young people. As examples, for those who are interested in being doctors or scientists, the understanding of opportunities in, for example, cancer research or disaster relief is not considered. Similarly, for those interested in gaming and programming, they may not be aware of the opportunities for the development of well-being or support apps in the charity sector. Or even the opportunities to lead a charity as a way to be a successful leader in a sector where you can make a difference, be innovative, and have a degree of flexibility and autonomy often not found in other sectors. Many know about the sector for volunteer opportunities or for the support it can offer, but not as a career option.

The fact that there is often no clarity of career progression and salaries don't always match other sectors could also be a barrier. Although I have heard it mentioned that when asked what they want to do with their lives, 80% of young people coming out of university say they want to make a difference in the world, they may just not think of the sector as a career option to do this.

In some ways, the charity sector, with its cross-organisational progressional routes, its supportive approach to staff, and its opportunity to make a difference, could fit well with the changing expectations of work.

This holistic approach to leaders' resilience, seeing it as something that effects the whole person and every part of their life, means that we need to take a much more holistic view of how we approach improving resilience. We should not focus on resilience at work alone. Any intervention to improve resilience needs to take a whole person approach too.

When I think about what were the key things leaders needed most from their peer support through acosvo, they included a safe space to learn and share, knowing it was okay not to get it right all the time, a sounding board, new ideas, somewhere they could feel safe to open up and say they didn't know the answer, and confirmation that they were doing the job okay. But they also needed to get to know each other a bit as individuals too. What could be seen as an old style of working, asking how the kids are, where you went on holiday, or how your hobby is progressing, was really important to underpin the safe space and the more human connections to allow sharing at a holistic leadership resilience level.

The other important dynamic for Third-Sector leaders is the Chair/CEO relationship and the exec/non-exec dynamic. This is an area which we haven't touched on too much so far but is interesting to consider during times of change. The power dynamic where the leader runs the organisation but the board oversees the governance is not always an easy one to navigate. Add in that it's a paid CEO role with a board of volunteers, often bringing experience from a wide range of sectors and specialisms, which means it can have its own challenges and complexities. The positive perspective is that these wide range of experiences could bring a diversity of thought and a wider concept and understanding of the changes to bring to the board table.

Research Relevance

This may be a good point to take the concept of the speed of change back to the learning from the research. If the main learning is that resilience is much more holistic and from a whole life perspective than previously considered, and that it's not just how we behave, but how we think and the environment around us that we have to take into account, how do we do this in an ever-changing world?

The holistic concept could be seen as both positive and negative. With more flexibility in how we work, it could be argued that it's easier to find time for the things we need to do to stay resilient. Whether that's time for family, leisure, peers, or other activities, we can surely fit this into the flexibility we now have. On the converse, does the "always on" world mean we never really switch off from work, always pick up the phone when it pings, and never fully immerse ourselves in the resilience activities we need so much to be able to recharge? Is our mindset impacted by trying to keep up with the changes and feeling like we are never doing enough, knowing enough, or connecting enough to really think about how we feel at our core? Finally, the environmental factors could feel overwhelming when we take into account the bigger picture of world challenges as well as keeping up with the speed of change within our workforce and workplace.

Summary

This chapter took us through the changing world of work and the emerging workforce. It considered the implications on our resilience and the way that we lead. It will now move on to reflect on the research, take the changing world into account, and consider how we develop new ways of working and practical application of this learning in the following chapters.

Resilience Reflections & Analogy: Change has Never Been So Fast But will Never be So Slow Again

This reminds me how important it is to keep up with the changes that are happening, or we will be left behind. It also highlights how important it is to continually think about your own resilience and how you must adapt and change your strategies as the world around us changes. Having said that, one of the things we often reminded sector leaders during the pandemic was that even when everything around you changes, your reason for being, to make a difference in the world, and the mission of your charity haven't changed – just the way in which you make it happen.

Reference

Grant, K., Egdell, V., & Vincent, D. (2021). *Young Peoples Expectations of Work and Workplace Readiness. Two Sides of the Same Coin.*

Chapter 7

Implications for Practice

No Such Thing as Bad Weather –
Only Inappropriate Clothing

Introduction

Working on the next few chapters reminded me about the importance of "finding your own voice" – and having the confidence to use it. I used to blog in my CEO role, very much my own thoughts from my own perspective. When I moved to academic writing, everything had to be referenced and validated. Now I find it a little harder to remember that I have my own voice from many years of experience both as a leader and working to support leaders for many years – as well as my years studying the subject of leadership and resilience. This chapter is where I put the academic learning together with my experiences and demonstrate ways to put learning from both into action. This has led to practical ways that we can all build and support our leadership resilience, no matter what sector or level of seniority we are leading from. They say that nothing is new; these models will no doubt be influenced by tools I have come across along the way. They are my own versions and interpretations, and I hope you find them useful.

My Resilience

My own resilience was challenged not long before I started this book. Soon after moving into my new position, I had reflected that it had come at a moment when I was having a bit of a wobble over the decision I had made to move on from my previous role. I had started to worry I was too young to "retire" and whether I would have enough money to live on. The new role sounded shiny and exciting – a new sector and new way of working – and, of course, I could fit it in (in the time I had carved out to finish my write-up of my thesis!).

As mentioned previously, I had agreed to take the role part-time for the first couple of months, quickly finding I would have to work full time – and more – to do it justice. I had a great team, very welcoming and supportive,

DOI: 10.4324/9781032627212-9

but the culture shock for me was real and took quite a while to adjust to. It was very strange no longer being the one who could do the job almost without thinking about it (unconscious competence), but who had to have support to navigate each task, decision, or project I wanted to carry out. A new sector, a new role, and a new team was maybe too much to take on while finalising my thesis and needing time for my parents. I soon realised I was spreading myself too thin and thus feeling very uncomfortable about not being able to do my best job at any of the things I was trying to do. Eventually, after eight months of trying my best and, in many respects, making good progress, I had to admit to myself that it had been the wrong thing at the wrong time and the role wasn't quite right for me at this stage in my journey. I should have stuck to my guns with my decision to focus on studies, writing, and occasional academic work and consultancy rather than get excited about "the next shiny thing". I handed in my notice, left on good terms with a new understanding of the public sector, and planned another exit.

Part two of my move to a "portfolio" career was approached with a bit more thoughtfulness and reflection, along with being wary of picking up too much work while I focused on my writing. I thought harder about the adjustments that had to be made in my life in terms of structure, expectations, and how to fill my days and still feel a sense of achievement. I reflected a lot on the "ikagi" (an ancient Japanese philosophy) principles of doing

- What you love
- What you're good at
- What you can be paid for
- What the world needs

For me, having a purpose was really important. Also finding the balance of doing things I love, which mostly focuses on people and making a difference in their lives – even if it's just making connections. One of my main fears of giving up my CEO role was losing my networks, which were very important to me – not just from a business perspective, but because these were the people I connected with who had common ground, language, and a shared sense of purpose. People I could rely on, whether it was just that I was in need of a coffee and chat, or some really good advice, new connections, or direction. I realised that I also benefitted from knowing they felt comfortable to reaching to me if needed too. These business networks are different from friendships, although some become friends at later stages in the journey.

Finally, I had to consider what effect my own ego had on the decisions I was making. It's quite an interesting psychological journey going from someone who has spent years building up a good reputation and level of respect to an unknown in a new way of working.

When moving into this new way of balancing a different kind of work and life, I initially really struggled with the lack of structure – be careful what you wish for! I thought it would be great to work to my own time-line and have total autonomy in the way that I work, but I really missed the structure as well as the people. I went through a phase when I couldn't make up my mind which things to focus on first – almost too much choice. Sometimes this meant my productivity slumped. I'd write endless lists of things I had to do, but with no set deadlines for some of the things I was working on, it was too easy to procrastinate.

I struggled to get used to having time to "do nice things", but then felt a lack of achievement and sometimes that I had "wasted time". It was probably from working at such a pace for so long, but it really did take quite a bit of adjusting, and I think I had definitely underestimated the culture shift I would experience. I didn't recognise that in many ways this was another "new world" I was exploring, but with less defined boundaries. Something I had dreamed of, but I hadn't realised I needed a mindset shift to come to terms with this new way of working. A new take on work-life balance when there is less "work" in the way that you have spent most of your life knowing it.

Implications for Practice

To consider the whole-life resilience concept shown through the shorthand of HLR = B + M + F, the diagram below shows how the intersection of behaviours, mindsets, and factors can lead to holistic leadership resilience (Figure 7.1).

Figure 7.1 Holistic Leadership Resilience.

Three Intersecting Circles Showing How Behaviours Mindsets and Factors Overlap to Show Holistic Leadership Resilience

This next section of this chapter takes the reader through how tools and concepts could be adapted to incorporate this thinking.

Practical Tools and Concepts

To squeeze in an extra analogy, a good workman (or a good leader) never blames his tools, but we'd be lost without a toolbox of useful ways to consider our resilience, and it was important for me to turn my learning into something practical that could be shared. In some ways an extension of the work I did to build connections and share across the many leaders in my network. When thinking about how I like to work and what has helped me along the way, I know I am very visual in the way I think and learn. I have drawn from my work on resilience when delivering workshops for leaders, and the section below will give some examples of exercises that allow a way to think through some of the concepts.

When I wrote my thesis, I reconceptualised a framework to consider my findings from the resilience of Third-Sector leaders. I also argued that the sector should have its own resilience framework rather than one reconceptualised elsewhere. I've developed a new version of the framework below based on the findings. It could be used in a number of ways, but first, let's look at simplifying the model I used in my thesis and making it more action-oriented (Table 7.1):

If, like me, you feel less is more, a quick tick list

1 **Connect:** Find your tribe's, support each other, share, and listen.
2 **Be Proactive:** Keep your resilience and wellbeing at the forefront – stay holistic in your thinking; learn what works for you.
3 **Balance:** Consider balance in all areas of life; be honest about your boundaries.
4 **Be you:** Be authentic, accept non-perfection, and know your strengths.
5 **Be passionate:** Build on passion and vision; do what you love.
6 **Be self-aware:** Have a holistic approach to life and work.

Okay, we've simplified the concepts to adapt to the time poor real world of life and work, but we still need to think about tools to help us when we get stuck. I've lost count of the number of times trusted colleagues have introduced me to a new tool or taken me through a reflective session. I've thought about what works for me and how they could be adapted or developed to incorporate the thinking on holistic leadership resilience. See which resonates with you.

Table 7.1 Holistic leadership resilience (adapted version)

Holistic Leadership Resilience

	Behaviour	Mindset	Factor

Connect
Support and learn
  from each other
	Offer support
	Find your tribe (s)
		Share
		Listen
			Gain support
			  from a wide
			  network
			And know the
			  importance of
			  wider support
			  network

Be Proactive
Consider
  well-being and
  put support in
  place
	Seek out support
	Understand what
	  works for you
		Reflect
		Learn
		  instinctive
		  passionate
			Understand wider
			  environment
			Be aware of
			  trigger points

Have balance
Understand the
  holistic nature
  of resilience
Be you
Focus on mission
  and impact
	Ensure balance
	  across all areas
	  of life
	Ask for help
	Accept
	  non-perfection
	Be authentic
		Balance adapting
		  and stability
		Be honest with
		  boundaries
		Have confidence
		Think ahead
		Make plans
			Be aware of
			  changing world
			Engage in all
			  directions
			Address issues
			Draw on
			  knowledge and
			  experience

Be passionate
Build on passion
  and vision
	Celebrate success
	Be persistent
		Be optimistic
		Accepting
		  of positive
		  feedback
			Show passion
			Hold the vision
			Understand the
			  context

Be self-aware
Has a holistic
  approach to
  well-being
	Acknowledge
	  importance
	  of non-work
	  activities
	Know when to
	  stop
		Self-aware
		Be honest about
		  what you need
			Understand
			  what can be
			  controlled
			Engage with all
			  areas of support

Climbing a Mountain

I've asked leaders to do a visual interpretation of what gets them through the day – what adds to their resilience and what takes away from it. My version uses an image of a mountain. It considers what helps you get up the mountain to achieve your goal and what drags you back down. I've seen lots of great versions of this – from huge wine glasses (what fills and what empties – a new version of glass half full!!) to beakers of resilience, to what gets you up in the morning and what keeps you awake at night. No matter how you visualise it (coloured pens at the ready), jot down examples from your daily life into two lists. What keeps you resilient and what drains your resilience? Even more helpful is if you do this over three mountains/ glasses/beds (see example below) to take into account the learning from the studies and consider which of those aspects are behaviours, which mindsets, and which factors. This helps to consider how (and whether) you can mitigate against the challenges.

Once you can see where your energisers and passions are in each area and where the things that drain your resilience are, you can start to think about how you might mitigate against the negatives and focus more on building the positives. What are the things you are passionate about that really energise you? (Example responses from my research were everything from playing with the kids, volunteering in a local group, having a leisurely bath, or going for a run and shutting out the world with your favourite tunes). If you know the things that drain you (competing requests, financial climate, difficult relationships, or just not enough time to do everything), at least you can look at those you might be able to move in the right direction or mitigate against, or even gain some acceptance of to help you along the way. Even if you just choose one of each to focus on and consider what you might do differently – and go back to any part of this book that resonated with you to help your thinking.

If you need to, use the elements from the study to spark your thinking, but don't let them confine you – it might be something else for you – we're all unique. Take time to work on each; be creative if that's your thing – write the words or draw what should be in there (Figure 7.2).

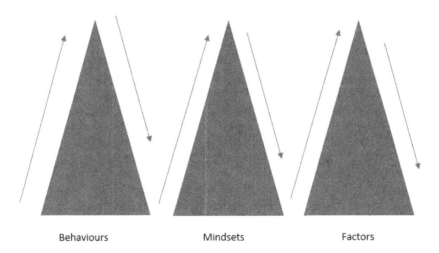

Behaviours   Mindsets   Factors

Figure 7.2 Mountain Exercise.

Three Mountain Shapes with Arrows up One Side and Down the Other

Once you have done this, you will have a greater understanding of where you get your resilience and what depletes it. This will help you focus on how you can build resilience (i.e., if going for a walk really helps, but you only do it once a week, how can you increase that to build more resilience?). Consider the things that drain your resilience, choose one to focus on, and think about what you could do to reduce the negative impact and stop the downward pull.

Remember, behaviours are things that you do, mindsets, the way that you think, and factors of the environment around you and how it impacts. If being outdoors improves your resilience, how can you get out more. If the funding landscape reduces your resilience, what could you do so it doesn't have such a big impact? This could be coming to terms with where funding is at and accepting you have to cut your cloth, or about being creative, widening the funding landscape, or finding innovating new ways to develop a funding pipeline; you are the only one who knows what can shift and what has to be come to terms with – but mitigated by other things that build your resilience.

Holistic Life Balance Grid

I first saw a version of this in "Feel the Fear and Do it Anyway" (Jeffers, 2017) much earlier in my career, but it still holds true. The more we have in our lives, the less impact it will have if one bit goes wrong. If we only have one key relationship and it breaks down, the hole in our lives is huge. If we have a wide social network, hobbies, friends, and are active in our local community, that impact could be lessened.

See which areas of your life might need some focus by filling in the boxes below with all the things that make up your life and how you spend your time.

Mapping life areas: Think about all parts of life and how you fill your time. Below is an example, but make the table as big or as little as you need. Do you feel you need more or less in your life? Should some squares be bigger than others? Make your own grid; add to the headings if it helps to give more detail (Table 7.2).

Once you have done this, take each area and consider behaviours, mindsets, and factors in each. Are there elements in each that help or hinder your resilience? Maybe try a red, amber, or green colour to see visually which gives you the most benefit – or are there different shades in elements of each? I'm purposely not being too prescriptive, as I think it's best if we adapt these examples in a way that works for us as individuals.

Table 7.2 Life map

Work	Home	Community
Friends	Leisure	Hobbies
Volunteering	Family	Neighbours
Colleagues	Exercise	study

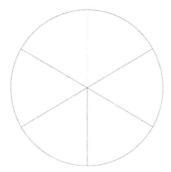

Figure 7.3 Wheel of Life.

Wheel of Life

Another tried and tested model that can be used in this way is the "wheel of life", often used in coaching. First, add each of the areas of life, for example, work, family, leisure, health, relationships, etc. Then think about how you rate your resilience in each, and then choose which one you really need to focus on to help you move forward. Rate each out of 10 in terms of your resilience, with the middle of the wheel being 0 and the circumference being 10 (Figure 7.3).

A Segmented Circle

Now, examine the completed diagram and see which areas you want to focus on. Again, consider behaviours, mindsets, and factors. You might want to do this yourself, work on it with a coach, or use it as a group exercise. The picture will help you see clearly which areas score lower than others and focus on where to put your energy to build your resilience.

Juggling

To go back to that concept mentioned earlier of leadership being like juggling while riding a unicycle. If we step off the unicycle for a moment and

Figure 7.4 Juggler.

focus on the balls we have in the air, it's important to consider which of those are rubber balls and would bounce if we dropped them, and which are glass and really need a lot of focus to keep them in place (Figure 7.4).

An Outline Picture of Someone Juggling

Take a sheet and draw the balls you are juggling. Fill each with the task that you are keeping in the air. Mark (or colour), which are rubber, and which are glass. Think about how your focus might be different for each. This exercise helps focus the mind on how best to spread your energy when there just isn't enough time to do everything you have in the air, never mind keep the unicycle upright and going in the right direction. Who could we throw some of these balls to lighten the load, and what ones can we leave to bounce and pick back up again later.

Vehicle

A version of another exercise I've used over the years involves drawing your leadership journey as a vehicle. Is it a beat-up car or a flashy supercar, a boat or spaceship...or something else. What is the path it is taking – a fast road full of potholes and obstacles? Where are you trying to get to? Are there other people in the vehicle? How far into the journey are you? Do you need to change your vehicle – every year, every five years? Maybe something to explore as part of a peer support group. Do the exercise individually, then talk your artwork through with trusted colleagues as a way to help see where you are in your journey and where you want to be. Look at it through the holistic lens. Are your resilience behaviours helping you drive safely, is your mindset making it an enjoyable journey, and what is the landscape like you are having to drive through?

Top Ten Resilience Tips from my Time as a Leader When the Going Gets Tough!

- Breathe.
- Drop your shoulders.
- Go outside, walk, stretch, and move.
- Write it down, everything; don't think; just get it out of your head.
- See friends, colleagues, and people you trust and can open up to.
- Set up a new group of peers – take the initiative.
- Try something new – you'll make mistakes and learn.
- Do something or be with someone to make you laugh.
- Cook, draw, do a task that you don't have to think about that's your passion, and get lost in the moment.
- Sleep – or if you can't.... go back to downloading from your brain – write, type, and speak it out.
- Remember, life is short; you only get one life; do what makes you happy ....
- Trust yourself – only you know what's best for you.
- It's okay to make it up as you go – it's what we're all doing.
- No such thing as imposter syndrome – fake it till you make it – there's only one you.
- Lose yourself in a book or watch a movie.
- Travel – somewhere you haven't been – anywhere.
- Be kind, help someone, and feel good all day knowing you have done something to help.
- Be friendly and smile.
- Take one step, no matter how tiny....

As I moved through my own succession journey, I put together a list of "top tips" of things to consider in the last 100 days in post. I have adapted this to be helpful for any change of direction in life when leaving one area to move to something new:

So, top tips for those heading to new adventures (and for the organisations they will be moving on from):

1 **Find Your "tribe":** I've gained hugely from peers who have gone through similar journeys before me. Having a sounding board can be incredibly helpful when having a wobble or just time out to think with trusted colleagues. It's also important to have colleagues at the same stage to go through the journey with. The importance of not feeling along is as pertinent at this stage of the journey as it is at the start.

2 **Support Your Team:** Whether a sigh of relief or a worry about what's next, don't underestimate the impact the pending change will have with your team (or family).

3 **Change Versus Stability:** There is a tendency to feel you need to "fix" everything before you move on. We want to leave things "in a good place", but knowing your successor will want to make their mark, think carefully about how much change to make happen before you go, and how much to leave to the next person.

4 **Networks:** Whether you want to disappear to travel the world or head off to another role, think carefully about your networks. Who do you not want to lose as a contact and how best to keep in touch.

5 **Recruiting Successor:** How should you be involved in recruiting your successor? I heard a spectrum of options, from "once you hand in your notice it's not your problem" to others who had sat alongside the board to give input on candidates and develop the job pack along the way. Work out what's right for you and your organisation. This applies whether it's a voluntary role, how you help a family member, or how you fill a gap when you make a change.

6 **Managing Your Ego:** No one is indispensable, and no one else cares about this as much as you do. It's important to understand this, but also to start to think about how it will feel not to be in your current role/situation. For many of us, we put all of ourselves into the roles we play, and it's important to think about dis-entangling and how you see yourself outside that role.

7 **Future Plans:** Once you make the decision to change direction, it can be a bit like a machine starts around you to make the process happen – and things get very busy. You've probably done a fair bit of thinking in advance, but make sure you find space to focus on what future you envisage and what post-role plans you need to put into place at the same time.

8 **Prepping to Go:** Think about what you are most proud of, memorable moments, etc. Take time to celebrate them. Develop a handover plan – identify "hotspots" for the person coming into the role. Think about what sits in your head – what intel do you need to share before you go – does it need to be written up? If you've been in the role a while, what's the organisational history that may be lost? Again, does this need to be recorded?

9 **Final Project:** Do you want to go out with a bang? Is there a final project you want to complete in this period? Do you have time? Think carefully about this one; it may lead to the next point.

10 **Stay Motivated:** It could be easy to say, "nothing matters now". Someone else will pick it up once I'm gone. Think about making the last 100 days impactful and what would make it feel like you are leaving things "in a good place", and a job well done will keep you focused.

11 **Go Gracefully:** No one needs you hanging about making things difficult for your successor. There are good arguments for handover

periods, and it can be tempting to keep a foot in the door. Tread carefully and work out what's best for both you and the organisation/situation.

12 **Emotional Impact:** Linking to the point on ego, don't underestimate the emotional impact the change could have. Leaving trusted colleagues or friends you have worked with over the years and often helped over the years see progress in their own journeys, the potential of losing networks you have built up over the years and moving on from being a respected and trusted leader/colleague, all take careful consideration. This could be lost along the way as the focus is on getting the organisation in the best shape for your move. We're only humans after all!

Summary

This chapter has considered practical tools and concepts to help leaders consider holistic leadership resilience in all areas of life. The next chapter will consider new ways to lead, incorporating some tried and tested concepts developed as part of my leadership journey.

Resilience Reflections & Analogy: No Such Thing as Bad Weather – Only Inappropriate Clothing

I link this analogy to how we see the environment we operate in. No matter how bad it is (or the weather gets), there are things we can do to mitigate the damage, and knowing ourselves and what works for us is where this thinking starts. As an example, I always like to walk a way along a path before I know if it's the right one, and if not, backtrack and try another. I'm also very visual in the way I think and kinaesthetic in the way I make plans and learn along the way. I need to move furniture; I can't just measure out the space and work it out on paper; I need to know how it will look and feel as a space.

Another concept that works for me is to "focus on the space between". It's something I learnt when challenging myself to learn to ride a motorbike after most of my life as a pillion passenger. When riding a motorbike, if going through a gate, a narrow opening, or avoiding an obstacle, you don't look at the obstacle but focus on the space in between where you want the bike to go. Riding a bike means using the whole body, not just turning the steering wheel. Your head leads on the direction and the body, and the bike follows. If you focus on the obstacle, you are more likely to hit it. I realise this is true in life too – focus on the space in between!

Finally, learning from my hip surgery: Sometimes your mental health is as important as your physical health, and if you only focus on one, to the detriment of the other, recovery slows. I realised this when I was very stressed about my folks but unable to do many of the things that build my resilience. There were days when I had to walk a bit further than I should have or even go over more challenging terrain to places that gave me solace. I remember walking along a woodland ledge with my crutches where one slip would have had me down a ravine, but I need to get to the beach at the end – my happy place, where I could lie in a hammock (a fishing net) and listen to the waves – to find some peace. It also gave me confidence in how much I could still do. It had risks attached, but my mental health at that moment trumped the risk to my physical health, and it was a choice and a risk I felt I had to make.

Reference

Jeffers, S. (2017). *Feel the Fear and Do it Anyway*. Vermillion.

Chapter 8

New Ways of Leading

*Every Journey Starts with
a Single Step*

Introduction

This chapter will consider some new ways of leading and will explore how they link back to my recent research. First, Active Leadership, which will consider new ways of accessing peer support, networking, and building relationships (i.e., it doesn't have to be behind a desk), then leadership exchange, a way to build learning, bust myths and understand leadership across and between sectors. Finally, we will consider the Interim Executive role and how it can be useful to help build organisational resilience. First, I'll give an update on my own resilience journey at this stage.

Resilience Journey

When writing this book, things didn't go quite to plan. For anyone thinking of doing something similar, think about how long it might take you and add six months of contingency! Back to "we make plans, and the gods laugh" (although I did make it by the deadline). During the year of writing, my parent's health started on a bit of a downward trajectory. It was no longer viable or safe for my mother to solely be the carer for my stepfather, even with a support plan in place. This led to an almost full-time job of finding a care home for my dad and sheltered housing for my mum. This would need to suit both their care needs and be close enough in proximity so my mum could still manage to visit my dad.

Surely, my job as CEO of a support organisation would stand me in good stead. All I can say is, for someone who thought they could find their way through any system, it turned out not to be the case. I went round in circles, came across stumbling blocks, filled in some things online, some on paper, and had to source so many supporting documents, but eventually, with the help of some amazing individuals within the system, managed to find suitable options for both parents. After taking a few seconds to congratulate myself…. I realised that my next task was to help to reduce

DOI: 10.4324/9781032627212-10

the family home they were leaving behind – with a million memories, keepsakes, and much-loved furniture – to a tiny bedroom in my dad's case and a one-bedroom apartment in my mum's – a much more physical, but no less demanding job with all the emotions attached.

This all took a toll on my own mental health. I wanted to be there for them, but had made quite a few commitments (to friends, to my husband, to consultancy work, and to this book), and I felt I didn't want to let anyone down. I felt guilty if I wasn't there as much as I should have been for my folks, but also that the plan to travel, change the way I lived my life, and have more leisure time became a distant dream. I didn't grudge a second of what I had to do, but I did feel I couldn't please all of the people all of the time – so similar to how I often felt at work, reinforcing my thinking on whole-life resilience.

So, where did I find my own resilience during this time? Well, my usual running and physical options fell by the wayside as my severe osteoarthritis meant I had to have a hip replacement. I was initially on crutches, not allowed to run for six months (my consultant would have preferred never, but I did find a sympathetic physiotherapist who agreed to help me get back to running). I realised a slow 5,000 km might be my limit, but that was enough. I was allowed to cycle though, and this came as a great relief. I thankfully recovered well but realised I'm not a good patient – with very little patience. I also realised how lucky I was to have the option to get the surgery done while I was otherwise pretty healthy and could have a quick recovery. Talking with friends and family helped – as ever, my peer support network came to the fore.

Once my folks were both settled for a few months in their new homes and I was recovered enough, we planned a much-needed holiday in the sun in a dark, cold Scotland. We hired bicycles for the week and were looking forward to a well-deserved break. Two days in, I got a call to say my dad had been rushed to the hospital and only had hours to live. On an island over five hours away with only two flights a week back home, this felt emotionally hugely challenging, as I just wanted to be there for them. I found that the best way for me to help was what I could do practically, by spending hours each day on phone calls to family and making arrangements. I did still manage to enjoy being away a bit, but it tore me in two not to be able to be there.

My daughter and my other younger brother came to the rescue, reminding me not to take it all on myself – a good reminder to ask for and accept help. When I called my daughter to let her know what was happening, she said she would follow my example from a time many years before when my son had an accident. She put fuel in the car and packed a bag and took it a step at a time but ended up being there when needed. The example she was referring to was when I heard my son was in an ambulance, had a head injury, had been unconscious, and more worryingly couldn't see. He was a couple of hours away, and I knew there was nothing I could do and I should wait until he was at the hospital to get an update on his condition. My daughter was young, and it was only the two of us at home. My son competed in BMX, was a young adult, and was with his girlfriend, but I couldn't sit still. "I said to my daughter, let's just go and fill the car in case we need to go. Why don't we pack a bag, just in case..." then, why don't we start driving, so if we are needed, we're not so far away (and we can always turn around if all is fine); of course, we kept driving and got there before getting an update, but we realised our help was needed and were so glad we had come. Although concussed and unable to walk, there wasn't a bed on a ward available. It was too far to go home, and he had to go back first thing next morning for more tests and checks, so at least I could organise a hotel room and help with anything that was needed. This lesson stuck with my daughter, and she slipped straight into it while wondering if my mum would need her in my absence. Don't underestimate the ripples you are making by the behaviours you are exhibiting.

This next section will take you through the new ways of leading, learning, and behaving that have been developed while working with Third-Sector leaders.

Active Leadership

As shown in the section on factors, the environment we work and live in influences our resilience. Many respondents also mentioned the activities that helped their resilience. Walking, being outdoors, and gardening – activities from gentle to extreme were all things with a positive impact. The benefits of being outdoors and in the fresh air are well documented. I've also found that having discussions side by side rather than face-on is much less confrontational and perfect for challenging conversations as well as peer support. We've also seen examples such as the "Outdoor Office" in the Netherlands (or "made by nature" desks), where the office is moved outside. This is now a growing international network of likeminded people who are spreading the word about the benefits of working outdoors.

I've mentioned in previous chapters some of the challenges with my own leadership resilience and how being active has helped. An example of a lesson I learnt from my charity bike ride across Nepal was the lesson of trusting the bike to find its own way. Something our guides encouraged us to do on the rocky terrain. The tyres were suited to the rough ground, and if we let them do their job rather than try to force a way, a natural route usually emerged. This trip also reminded me that knowing when to stop and take time to rest and when to dig in and push on is really important.

Adjusting our pace to the altitude was a good example of taking the factors or environment into account.

But how does this all this thinking align with strong leadership, learning, and the essentials of peer support and its role in resilience, and how did I put it into some kind of practice?

While working with leaders, I developed an "Active Leadership Programme". We tried everything from walking to cycling, kayaking, and wild swimming, all proving very beneficial. One interesting challenge was the perceptions of others. I remember one leader telling me she had to take a half day from her annual leave as she "couldn't been see to be off on a cycling jolly" when she should be working. This thinking does need a bit of exploring. Why is it okay to sit around a board table, discuss leadership concepts, offer peer support, learn from each other, and build our networks and connections and possible opportunities to work together – but not to do it in a heathier way.

How Did It Work?

We started with walking and using some structure. We asked participants to come along with their "wicked Issues" (Grint, 2010) sturdy footwear and dressed for the Scottish weather (all eventualities). After gathering together and doing introductions and a little bit of a background on the benefits of being outdoors and active, we started on the walk (on a quiet cycle/canal path for around 10,000 km). Participants paired up to walk and talk and take turns to discuss their issues and get to know each other. We stopped at appropriate points and switched pairs to enable as many perspectives on the issues as possible. There was also the opportunity to walk alone for a while and reflect on what we had been discussing and what the implications might be.

At the end of the walk, we all congregated for a well-earned cuppa and discussed how we had found it. I remember one participant telling me it felt like they had benefitted from four different perspectives on their issue and could see a way forward – and had offers of help and connections along the way. They also appreciated the opportunity to be outside, enjoy the fresh air, and do something very productive (and cost-neutral – no consultancy fee or booking a board room) along the way.

We developed the walks in different ways, from less structured and having stops for discussion and leaving groups to form along the way on similar topics to walks with specific purpose (e.g., foraging, exploring different environments, visiting different areas and projects, and having input along the way).

It was a little trickier for the cycling. Safe cycle paths and wide canal paths were really important so we could ride side by side. Stopping to enjoy the environment and having bigger group chats along the way helped too. We did find we could hold conversations in pairs as we cycled, and the occasional moves to single file helped reflection as much as stuttered the discussion.

Kayaking was more of a team activity but had many of the same results. By the time everyone had donned their wetsuits and figured out what they were doing, they had gelled pretty well. For experienced Chief Executives used to being in their comfort zone (for some, kayaking was a new experience) – with the fear factor heightening the senses, peer support and encouragement were more important than ever. It also gave the more experienced the chance to offer practical support. Having instructors give us the chance to experiment and gain confidence quite quickly also added to the excitement. Getting into teams and playing "water football" gave a healthy challenge – and a lot of fun – and brought out the competitive spirit rarely lacking in a group of leaders. But this wasn't team building for individuals to get to know each other and work better together. It was an alternative way to quickly build connections, share confidences and concerns, and build trust to be able to share and discuss challenges as leaders. The buzz over lunch afterwards certainly showed the benefits. Although not the same opportunity to go deeply into issues, I saw many swapping details to follow up on things they had touched on and a shared spirit of support and understanding.

Wild swimming was again a different opportunity in a different way. We came together at a remote loch and had brought an experienced "trainer" to keep us safe and make sure everyone had the basics. Similar to kayaking, the mix of nerves for the newbies and excitement for more experienced wild swimmers brought a buzz to the day. Not something you would normally find a group of CEOs doing together, but lots of analogies to our day jobs around assessing risks, looking after each other, and pushing ourselves to see how much we could achieve. The bonding and sense of achievement and team spirit, along with the cakes and hot chocolate, also added to the peer support and network building.

It should be said that all of these sessions (which became an established part of our offers) were all led by charity leaders working in the field of the specific activity (e.g., Cycling Scotland, Paths for All, etc. – big thanks to all those who helped us along the way).

This next section will consider another new way of leading, Leadership Exchanges, to help us lead across sectors and geographies with a greater understanding of each other's cultures and languages.

Leadership Exchange

I've touched on Cultural Intelligence (CQ) previously, but here it comes to the fore (Middleton, 2016). This concept is a move on from Intelligence Quotient (IQ) and subsequently emotional intelligence (EQ) (Goldman,

2007). CQ is defined as the ability to cross divides and thrive in multiple cultures. This doesn't just mean geographical cultures, but sectoral, generational, and cultures of faith and beliefs. If we can truly "walk in each other's shoes" and really understand each other's perspectives. Julia's work considers "core" and "flex". How much of ourselves do we have to hold on to be true to ourselves, and how much can we flex to take others' perspectives into account and to truly understand where they are coming from? I was privileged to see this at work firsthand on a visit to Malaysia as part of a Common Purpose (founded by Julia Middleton) programme, The Commonwealth Study Conference, which brought together participants from across the commonwealth for a global leadership programme.

The initial idea of the Leadership Exchange Programme I developed at acosvo came from international exchanges I had taken part in through being a longstanding member of the Euclid Network. I had the privilege to take part in many different exchanges over the years with leaders from Serbia, Russia, Catalonia, and Sweden. The programme allowed peers to learn together through exchange visits and was a chance to share best practice and learning, gain a fresh perspective in a different environment, challenge our thinking, encourage collaborative working, build new relationships, and discuss future plans and strategy with another leader from a different environment. All of the exchanges worked both ways – as well as visiting other projects and organisations, we also hosted them back in Scotland on a reciprocal visit. The ethos of those peer exchanges was all about the sharing of knowledge and building bridges between our understanding, our learning, and our connections. We would plan the exchanges to meet our objectives and to give as wide an immersion of understanding as possible. I've said from previous exchanges that I learn as much from seeing my own world through the eyes of others as I do from exploring a new world.

I was often struck by how open and welcoming everyone I met on my journeys was. All were as keen to listen, learn, and understand as I was, and were very generous in the time they committed to do that. On all the exchanges, I got to visit a range of projects, get some background into how the exchange partners worked, the culture and environments they worked in, and the challenges and opportunities they faced in their roles – and also get to know them as people and as leaders. You may not be surprised to find that even in a very different context, there were not as many differences as you would expect. The exchanges also covered a more social aspect, partly to understand the culture and environment we each worked in and to build bonds and trust to help us share as leaders.

On all of my exchanges, I left full of thoughts and ideas to ponder, strong connections in a new area, and motivation to remember the importance of walking in another's shoes and seeing your world through new eyes.

While in my role working with Third-Sector leaders in Scotland, I pondered how this learning might work across different sectors and not just geographical boundaries. A colleague (shout out Laurena Charles[1]) and I developed a Leadership Exchange Programme that paired leaders at middle, senior, and executive levels to offer them brief cross-sector exchanges, gaining an insight into a different world of work. The pilot programme matched leaders within government with those within the Third Sector. The purpose was to provide a bridge for cross-sector knowledge sharing where leaders could gain insight into the different cultures, languages, constraints, and opportunities their counterparts work with. The hope was to build a greater understanding and a move towards more collaborative working. We soon found that many peers continued to meet after the exchange was complete (we suggested a commitment of at least six months), build bonds and connections, and act as that bridge between sectors across a wider spectrum than just as individuals. As a very brief explanation of how they worked, leaders completed a short application form detailing their role and an area of work they wanted to focus on (e.g., strategy, governance, people management, etc.) and were matched with someone with similar criteria. They committed to working together over six months, getting to know each other, spending time in each other's workplaces, and sometimes observing (or taking part in) meetings and events.

The success of this pilot then developed into a wider exchange programme across all sectors, with a significant number of leaders having the opportunity to walk in the shoes of another and see their world through new eyes. When I moved into academia, I mentioned previously that I had to learn a new language, and when into the health service, a new culture and new systems. It could be argued that as career paths are less linear than in the past, this shouldn't be such a rarity, but in a time when collaborative working can be seen as key to meeting some of our wider ambitions (from addressing climate change to pooling our resources to make a difference in people's lives). Leaders matched across all sectors can be seen as a unique opportunity to expand their network, see things differently, and build connections across boundaries. Another element I came across in all of the exchanges was around dispelling myths. I've lost count of the times I've been totally wrong about how I thought things were on the other side of the fence – and I've seen eyes open wide in surprise when leaders from other sectors have been surprised at how we work in the Third Sector – the complexity of the triple bottom line and the business acumen needed to make a difference.

I remember a Third-Sector leader saying that when they looked at how to stay afloat in difficult times, they looked at business news sections to see what was happening elsewhere and took into account when making own plans – how many private sector organisations look to charities to see what they could learn? There are many "businesspeople" on Third-Sector boards, but not so many Third-Sector people on private and public sector boards or even on academic "courts".

Interim Executive

As mentioned previously, the Third Sector had gone through a challenging time. Many sector leaders were considering moving on from their role. This wasn't just due to burnout because of the pressures, although I'm sure that had a part to play. The age demographic and the changing expectations of work-life balance after the pandemic also had a part to play. We had become aware of an area our counterparts in Northern Ireland were exploring – how "interim" CEO's may be a new service that could be offered when organisations found themselves needing support or without a CEO. We had the opportunity to join in some of the training (shout out, Dr. John Brothers[2]), and the interesting concept of being "pre-fired". This means that for a leader coming in for a fixed term with a set objective, they are "pre-fired" and can do some of the difficult "turnaround" work if needed as they know they are not in it for the long term. They may also be involved in hiring their successor.

The service that was developed provides voluntary sector organisations, boards, and outgoing CEOs tailored access to expert, experienced voluntary sector Interim Executives. The service could be used to bridge a temporary gap in leadership, as a support to the CEO or senior staff, or Board members in times of need or change, or for short-term focused assistance with key projects. Those that fulfil this interim role were all vetted as experienced CEOs in the sector with a range of skills to offer. ACOSVO purely not only acted as a matching service but also delivered training for the interim role based on the learnings from Dr John Brothers.

Some of the tasks Interim Executives could be asked to carry out included: transition management and recruitment support, crisis support and management, consultancy support, strategic reviews, maternity cover, organisational closure, succession planning, restructuring, and mergers and acquisitions. A peer support group for interims was also set up to enable the opportunity to share and learn from others in the role and consider best practice. As with Leadership Exchanges, the process was kept simple, with a brief "application" from the organisation to clarify the need, which was then matched with an interim's expertise in that area. The organisation was then connected with up to three possible matches, and it was up to them to go through a process of choosing who they wanted to work with and how they took the work forward.

This support has proved hugely valuable and has developed to meet the needs of the fast-moving environment and the increasing turnover in the leadership role. It's also suited the way of working that many of our experienced leaders who moved out of the Chief Executive role were keen to move on to. They could work intensively for shorter periods of time in areas where they could use their expertise and skills, but then take time to rest and recuperate before moving onto the next one. It could be argued that when not as "invested" in the organisation as they would have been as a long-standing Chief Executive, the drain on their emotional investment was not so great, and they could see the results of their efforts much more quickly as they completed the task in hand and moved the organisation on to the next stage.

Summary

This chapter has explored some new ways of leading and how they link back to my research. The concepts of Active Leadership, Leadership Exchange, and the Interim Executive role are all examples of concepts that have been trialled and developed in my previous role. They have shown new ways of leading and linking to our new environment that we work in and the need for more cross-sector learning to enable partnership working with a real understanding of each other's sectors.

Resilience Reflections & Analogy: Every Journey Starts with One Step

I've said previously that I have to walk along a path before I know if it feels like the right one; this analogy picks up on that. If you stand still with a few different paths or options ahead of you, it's easy to get stuck in a decision-making crisis. I've found that I have to start to walk along a path (or drive in a direction, as mentioned at the start of this chapter) before I can tell if it's the right one. If not, I can quickly retrace my steps and try the next one. I did find that at one stage this way of working drove my team mad as I shared some of my ideas and thinking as I went up one path, then backtracked and started going along another. I quickly realised that I had to be much clearer about when I was "exploring" and "trying things out" and when I was actually making a decision to head in that direction.

To pick up the analogy from a different "direction", hillwalking always comes to mind. You are still moving towards your goal (the top of the hill – or the safety of the bottom), as long as you are putting one foot after the other. One of my experienced hillwalking friends once said, no matter how exhausted you are, as long as you can take one more step, then just one more step, you'll get there. I've had some of my best thinking and best ideas (as well as my mad ones) when on a hill. It's a mixture of relying on colleagues to keep each other safe, build bonds, and share ideas, and lots of time with your eyes on the path and checking the terrain while your mind can go elsewhere and start to make sense of things all on its own (and much healthier that it is doing it at 3am when you really need to sleep!).

It can also be when constructive challenge, listening skills, and making informed decisions come to the fore – especially when everyone in the group has a different opinion on the way off the hill when the mist comes down. The sense of shared achievement also adds to building trust and relationships. The lesson of only going at the speed of the slowest person to keep everyone in the group together is a good reminder too (or allocating "scouts" to check out the way ahead).

I'm also very aware of the balance of physical and mental health. I remember after my hip surgery needing to get to my "happy place" – a hammock on the beach where I can listen to the waves and chill out (no matter what the weather), but realising it was a bit treacherous track to get though on crutches! I did make the decision that it was worth the risk and took the first step – knowing yourself was a mindset that definitely came to the fore.

Finally, think back to the start of this chapter, when my daughter followed my example of, just taking one step towards solving a problem when you're not sure if it needs your attention yet. If it helps you be in the right time at the right place to take action when needed, it's definitely a journey worth considering.

Notes

1 https://www.linkedin.com/in/laurena-charles-64a99a12/
2 https://www.linkedin.com/in/drjohnbrothers/

References

Goldman, D. (2007). *Emotional Intelligence*. Bloomsburry Publishing.
Grint, K. (2010). Wicked Problems and Clumsy Solutions: The Role of Leadership BT. In S. Brookes & K. Grint (Eds.) *The New Public Leadership Challenge* (pp. 169–186). Palgrave Macmillan UK. https://doi.org/10.1057/9780230277953_11
Middleton, J. (2016). *Cultural Intelligence*. Bloomsbury Academic.

Chapter 9

The Way Forward

Each Destination is But a Doorway to Another Journey

Introduction

This final chapter will summarise the learning on leadership from my research, from my own resilience journey, and from my time as a leader. It will also look at how this learning is relevant across all sectors. The different stages of leadership journeys will also be explored, i.e., what it means for new leaders as they develop and how it could also be helpful for those coming to the end of their formal leadership journeys.

Finally, it will consider what areas of research may be relevant for future exploration.

My Resilience

At the final stage of writing this book, in some ways I'm as busy as ever. I've joined a voluntary sector board, and I'm still working out how to best balance my time between geographies and family. I've also been doing bits of consultancy work, speaking gigs, and connecting with colleagues. I'm still working out what "structure" means for me when I no longer have a "working week" or have to be at my desk at a set time. It's an absolute privilege to be in this position, and I don't take it lightly, but it definitely turns the world on its head a little. Am I a person who wants to write for a couple of hours every morning/evening – or do I have to be "in the mood"? There is still something about knowing yourself and knowing what works for you. I'm also much more aware of the role "ego" plays in some of the decisions I make. It takes time to get used to the fact that you are no longer responsible for everyone around you, and you have to earn respect in a different way. People see you differently, and from a world where you might be seen as a respected leader (I'm hoping I was) to "the retired older woman", can be a bit strange. Part of me loves the fact that I can take two hours to walk to the shops from my island home (it should take 30 minutes), as I have time to stop and chat and pass the time of day, but after a

DOI: 10.4324/9781032627212-11

lifetime of deadlines, I still get disappointed if I don't feel I have achieved as much as I think I should.

I struggle with feeling the pressure of finding a new version of myself as not a CEO and not in employment. How do I support my mother while respecting her independence and living my own life? Even finding a new way of being as a "retired" couple and deciding how we will spend our time has taken a lot of headspace. I'm also aware that changing status and how I see myself and how others see me is all ego-based and something I must explore further to come to terms with.

On a practical basis, I'm planning to up sticks and move to my island home. My husband has taken up sailing, my new hip is settling in, and I'm back to jogging (not sure I can call it running at the pace I now go at)! I'm delighted to be able to get back in the hills, and I'm exploring what other opportunities are out there – but I might need a break first. One thing I do know is that I still need the occasional mad adventure to keep me from getting bored and to continue to challenge and stretch me, but I can hopefully do so with a better understanding of my own resilience – partly due to the process of writing this book and considering what it means to me, alongside the research from my studies.

...and just as I am finishing this book, the gods laugh at my plans again, with the lovely news that I am going to be a grandmother. As my daughter stays five hours away from my island home and we both want me to be around more, I might just have to rethink....

Research Round Up

This next section will round up the research findings and start to consider what it means for leaders across all sectors. It will first slip back into the "academic" style of writing to complete the aim of showing the outcome of academic research while linking to the practical applications, so it will aim to be of interest to both academics, potential academics, and practitioners (although I hate to put people in boxes, and we are all probably an amalgamation of all those roles – pracademic being a useful, but not my favourite, term).

The aim of this research was to explore behaviours that may influence and improve resilience for Third-Sector leadership. A social constructivist, interpretive approach was used, which aligned with the method of semi-structured interviews and the "no one truth" approach that resilience is a concept that means something different to each individual. Although this was borne out through the breadth of the findings, there were key themes that could be analysed to draw out the main concepts of resilience and behaviours that came through from both the literature and the interview findings. These were presented through an extended and reconceptualised framework that may improve resilience in Third-Sector leadership and beyond. This has been developed and visually constructed in an accessible form and has led to the adaptation of practical tools and a better understanding of resilience behaviours in Third-Sector leadership, which could be transferable across sectors.

During the research, it became apparent that the speed of change and the ways of working have evolved so much over the last few years, even without taking the pandemic into account, that much of the literature is based on a different concept of work-life balance. The fact that a large proportion of leaders work virtually now and that the working day is no longer bounded by traditional working hours means that a reconceptualising of both the concept of resilience and the behaviours, factors, and mindsets involved need to be considered in a more holistic manner to gain both a wider and deeper understanding of the concepts.

This next section will look at what this means as a contribution to knowledge and then follow with the contribution to practice.

Contribution to Knowledge

The research resulted in two substantive findings. It showed that resilience is more "holistic" than generally explained in the literature. Although the literature recognises that key relationships and support have a big part to play, the concept that all elements of life impact resilience and that resilience at work and resilience as a leader do not stand alone from resilience in wider life is not strongly ascertained.

The other key finding is that exploring behaviours alone is not enough to get an in-depth understanding of resilience. Although the questions asked were on perceived behaviours, some of the answers given could be characterised as mindsets and factors. All three aspects have to be taken into account. The following sections will look at each of these aspects in turn before summarising what this means as a contribution to knowledge.

The first question of the study explored what resilience meant to participants as Third-Sector leaders. The expectation was that because the question was asked in the context of their role, the answer would be work-based and related to their role as a leader. The findings highlighted a range of themes, which implied that resilience was seen as an element that was important across all aspects of life and was not only discussed from a work perspective.

The importance of knowing where to find support and to build networks across all areas of life came through strongly. The human aspects of resilience were also prevalent and evidenced through the importance of values, trust, impact, and kindness, which were all seen as keys to resilience. Adapting to change and continuing to evolve was a further theme.

The theme of "self" had a wide range of aspects, from knowing oneself, acknowledging and understanding energy levels, being aware of limitations, and not taking things personally.

Participants gave examples of what resilience meant to them from all areas of life, discussing who they were as a person, what works for them to keep them resilient, and what networks need to be in place to support them when needed. The role of the leader and the stresses involved were acknowledged, but the understanding of resilience and the way it was discussed was across a much wider scope than purely within a work setting.

The three key behaviour themes that influence and improve resilience were identified from the research as: holistic, acceptance, non-perfection, and peer support.

Holistic leadership behaviours were identified as non-work activities, work/life balance, family/friends, and being human. This holistic way of behaving, of not seeing only work behaviours as those that influence and improve resilience, was a key finding from this research, which could have implications for both future research and current thinking on the topic.

The behaviour of acceptance of non-perfection, being able to try new things, not being afraid to fail and to learn from the experience, and not always having to get things right the first time could be seen as vital in today's changing and evolving world of work.

The behaviours that incorporate and encourage peer support were also seen as essential as a way to influence and improve resilience in Third-Sector leaders who often feel lonely in the role.

Each of these behaviours was explored in more detail in the previous chapters, but the overarching understanding was that these were the key behaviours that came out most strongly and gave a clear picture of what the more holistic behaviours are that influence and improve resilience in Third-Sector leadership.

Alongside behaviours, the responses from the research identified that mindsets and factors also had a part to play in influencing and improving the resilience of Third-Sector leaders.

The most prevalent mindset identified incorporated elements of "self". This included being self-aware, having self-belief, practicing self-reflection, considering self-care, knowing yourself, and benefiting from positive feedback. Other key elements that were identified included having a learning mindset, having confidence, and being optimistic. This has shown that leaders have to have a much wider view of what influences and improves their resilience than previously understood. Much of the literature explored did not include mindsets as an element of resilient leadership, or if it did so, did not connect it to the bigger picture alongside behaviours and factors as a concept of holistic resilience.

The most prevalent factors identified were governance, context, trigger points, and exhaustion. The part the governing board has to play, the context leaders are working in, the trigger points they need to be aware of, and the exhaustion they were suffering from at the time of interviews all contributed to influencing and improving resilience. It was also interesting that responses to how leaders understood resilience also resulted in factors being mentioned. These included the information they had available, the experience they brought to the role, and what sort of control they had of the situation. Much of the literature explored did not identify the factors that influenced and improved resilience alongside the behaviours and mindsets and thus did not consider the more holistic resilience thinking that has resulted from this research. When writing a doctoral thesis, we have to conclude by considering what the contribution of the learning is to both knowledge and practice in the field.

This contribution to knowledge is important as it could lead to a new understanding of the wider concepts of resilience. It incorporates the changing, more turbulent world we live and work in and could influence and inspire further exploration of the theme by future research.

The reconceptualised framework could influence how the Third Sector is seen and understood both by researchers and by other sectors. The fact that there are similarities between Third Sector leaders and high-flyers in the corporate sector is a concept that may not have been previously explored. The wider understanding of resilience, alongside the identification of the holistic behaviours that influence and improve it, contributes to knowledge by adding an additional element, "holistic", and a wider context, the Third Sector, which is rarely included in business research. In today's world of "triple bottom line" of people, planet, and profit (Elkington, 1997), the Third Sector could be seen as leading the way in this new thinking around holistic leadership resilience.

We'll now move on to consider the contribution to practice.

Contribution to Practice

The study contributed to practice by exploring and potentially extending how resilience is considered by Third-Sector leaders. When previously it may have been seen solely as a "work" issue, the study contributed not only to the understanding of the role that those other areas of life have to play, both in terms of adding to stressors, but also as a way of influencing, improving, and thus building more holistic resilience.

It developed a reconceptualised framework that will have an impact on how leaders in the Third Sector (and potentially beyond) think about their resilience and what actions they may take to improve it. The work has also offered a practitioner shorthand to help aid the understanding of leadership resilience. This work may thus inform practice (as shown in previous chapters), could lead to further research, and has led to the development of tools and techniques to improve resilience for Third-Sector leaders.

As discussed previously, the finding that participants understood resilience from all areas of life could lead to a contribution to practice from the understanding of where both threats to resilience and ways to build resilience can be found. This means that when developing support for leaders, the wider, more holistic ways they live their lives should be taken into account. Building good support networks may start to be seen as not something that only needs to be considered in a work environment, but that social support networks are also important. It could also mean that more support could be considered for leaders going through difficult times in family life, as it will impact their role as a leader. This understanding could lead to support being developed that would take all aspects of the leader into account and not just the elements seen as related to their working life. This practice contribution could have implications on how leaders are recruited, how they are supported, how their working lives are "balanced", and subsequently how they lead both their people and their organisations. It could also have implications for how we support and mentor aspiring leaders through the succession pipeline.

As mentioned in the previous section, the three key behavioural themes that influence and improve resilience were identified from this research as holistic, acceptance, non-perfection, and peer support. From a practice perspective, this means that a much more holistic approach can be taken to practice. Considering resilience behaviours and tools and frameworks that support these behaviours will no longer only take into account behaviours and ways of doing things at work but can incorporate all aspects of life.

The understanding of acceptance of non-perfection as a resilience behaviour could be developed into training for both new and established leaders and managers. This would mean that the ability to try new things, adapt, and change to circumstance and the development of a culture that doesn't apportion blame onto failure but sees it as a way to learn and innovate can be cultivated.

The importance of peer support to improving resilience could be nurtured, developed, and more widely recognised. Developing relationships can sometimes be seen as a luxury when the focus is internal for leaders in difficult times. Knowing that it is important to develop a wide range of peer support networks to thrive gives credibility to the need to focus time and energy on building these networks.

Also mentioned in the previous section, the responses from this research identified that mindsets and factors had a part to play in influencing and improving the resilience of Third-Sector leaders.

The identification of mindsets as an influencing factor in improving resilience means an enhanced understanding of this concept and the potential for the development of both emotional intelligence and cultural intelligence as being key to improving resilience. How leaders think in addition to how they act will be incorporated into thinking and consequently into how tools and models are developed and used in support and training of Third-Sector leaders.

The identification of wider factors and the context that leaders operate within and the impact both have on resilience are also important. Leaders will not only look inward at what is impacting their resilience but will have gained a better understanding of the external factors that are impacting their resilience. There may be a better understanding of the impact of considering what is and what is not within their control and how learning and strength can be drawn from other areas of life.

This contribution to practice is important as it could lead to new ways of working and the development of new and reconceptualised models and tools. The reconceptualised framework developed from this research could influence the advancement of these models and tools by giving a clear indication of the behaviours to be taken into account. It will make a contribution by widening the practical understanding of the wider concepts of resilience, both for current and emerging leaders. This may lead to a reduction in burnout and thus more resilient leaders. The identification of holistic resilient behaviours and the importance of mindsets and factors in the equation will mean that the way leaders are trained, developed, and supported through face-to-face learning, development tools, literature, and training methods may all benefit from this understanding.

Summary of Contributions to Knowledge and Practice

Through these findings, this study has contributed to the extending and widening of the concept of resilience in Third-Sector leadership with the lessons that could resonate across all sectors. It has also identified and explored what part behaviours, mindsets, and factors have to play in the equation. Participants have come from the position of leadership, with the act of leadership being explored through behaviours. The motivations of Third-Sector leaders have also been considered. With all these aspects taken into account, it has reconceptualised a framework that was designed for highflyers in the private sector to be relevant to Third-Sector leaders in the way they think about resilience and their own wellbeing as leaders. It incorporates a wider view of what areas of life and work impact a leader's resilience and gives a range of areas for consideration on building resilience in Third-Sector leadership.

The study also incorporated the changing world we live and work in and what this may mean in relation to studies and learning from previous periods. It tells us something new about leaders and the support they need to improve and influence their resilience and fills a gap in both knowledge and practice. This work is potentially applicable and transferrable across countries and jurisdictions with similar governing systems, and possibly more widely across geographies. It could also have implications for cross-sector collaborative leadership by improving understanding of what influences and improves resilience across different sectors, thus potentially aiding leaders understanding of how best to work together and support each other in their leadership roles.

Strengths of Study

That the study was conducted within the Third Sector is a strength, as is the fact that it focused on leadership in Scotland. In general, the majority of research on leadership is conducted in the United States and focuses on the world of business. It is generally less common for Third-Sector organisations to be the focal point of research in the leadership field.

The in-depth nature of the research, the interpretive approach taken, and the sector knowledge and understanding of the researcher could also be seen as strengths. These elements mean that the research has been carried out "by" the sector, for the sector, and with the sector and could thus give it more credibility and a greater likelihood of it being incorporated into practice.

The managerialist approach and output, alongside the potential for practical implications, can also be seen as a strength that could build on sector leaders' ability to both understand and improve resilience. The potential for current tools, models, and approaches to use the findings and the reconceptualised framework to consider how they can be adopted to incorporate this approach is significant. There is also the potential for new practical tools to be developed to incorporate the findings and be used with leaders in the sector to influence and improve their resilience.

Limitations of Study

As with any study, there are always ways that could be improved or done differently with hindsight and are worth consideration. The breadth of the focus could be seen as a limitation to the research. The sample size, the size of charities chosen, the time in post of the leader, the general nature of the wider sector, whether urban or rural, and whether gender, age, or background of the leader could all be seen as aspects that, when considered in more detail, could have implications on the findings and thus the impact on the sector and its leaders.

The literature considered focused on leadership and resilience, and it could be argued that a wider consideration of behavioural science may have taken the research in a different direction and explored specific behaviours, why they occur, and how they impact resilience. Conducting this research out with the period of the pandemic may have given a different insight, but the pace of change in so many other areas of working life may mitigate this consideration.

Future Research

There may be merit in expanding this research to include a comparison with other sectors. This could consider if the changing world of work, as it becomes more flexible and possibly more turbulent, contributes to a similar holistic expansion of how resilience is identified and thus the behaviours, mindsets, and factors that have been found in this research.

There is also scope in exploring, considering, and developing both reconceptualised and new models, tools, frameworks, and guidelines specifically for Third-Sector leadership as an expansion of this research.

Any of the limitations detailed in the previous section could also be addressed by future research to explore the specific areas mentioned (the sample size, the size of charities, the time in post of the leader, the influence of place (e.g., urban or rural), gender, age, or background of the leader). The specialism of the sector could also be a consideration. Are leaders in the Environmental, Children's, Health, or Housing subsectors more resilient, for example? This could prove a useful way of identifying areas where learning could be shared and better understood between different contingents of the sector.

Whether there are specific aspects of being based in Scotland that have an impact on resilience could also be of interest to explore.

A further aspect for potential future research would be to consider how senior managers and governing bodies view the resilience of their Chief Officers. For senior managers, whether they recognise potential for burnout in their leaders, whether tools could be developed to help this identification, and what this might mean for themselves as aspiring leaders as they consider moving into the roles. From the study mentioned at the start of this book, which identified that almost 50% of leaders plan to leave their role within the next five years, how to support new leaders, aspiring or early career leaders in their role could be an important aspect for further consideration. For governing bodies or boards of trustees, a deeper understanding of resilience behaviours and how best to support their Chief Officer would also be a valuable resource.

An objective of the research was to "develop insights and recommendations which may improve resilience for Third Sector leadership". To meet this aim, the insights that have been drawn from the research have been incorporated into the recommendations that follow.

Insights and Recommendations

The recommendations that arise from this research can be split into three areas: the literature that pertains to the sector, the conceptual frameworks that are used, and the learning both within and across sectors that can come from this research. In addition to being separate recommendations, consideration should also be given to the collective recommendation that sits across all three: that the literature, conceptual frameworks, and practical learning and application all need further attention in relation to Third-Sector leadership. Finally, the importance of taking into account the changing work of work in relation to all of these recommendations is necessary for the desired outcome of influencing and improving resilience in Third-Sector leadership to be fulfilled.

Literature

When considering resilience through the lens of Third-Sector leadership, caution should be taken when using literature from other sectors. Although many areas co-relate and are relevant, a wider understanding of the sector and more academic literature are needed to underpin the credibility of future research. Thus, there is a recommendation that more research could be carried out specific to the Third Sector, and that incorporates the Third Sector. How this is funded, where the focus could be, and what outputs are needed should be developed in partnership between academic institutions and the sector itself. Examples of good practice could be explored to develop this work.

There is also a call for more research from the Third Sector to be recognised. A recent guide offers a framework for building trustworthiness into sector research (Bonetree et al., 2022). It is also a recommendation that more cross-sector work could be developed in this area. Work across the private, public, Third Sector, and academic world could lead to a better understanding of resilience for all leaders across sectors.

Conceptual Frameworks

When considering conceptual frameworks to support and develop practice, similar caution should be taken. Rather than being adapted to suit the Third Sector, this book has now developed a conceptual framework specifically for their needs that takes their specific context into account. Only by developing frameworks specific to the needs of Third Sector leaders can the insights and understanding of what resilience means to them and how to improve it can be properly understood.

This Third-Sector-specific framework could now be considered for suitability and adaptation for use in other sectors with similar motivations. This shared understanding could also aid collaborative working between sectors as we move towards a more holistic future.

These frameworks have also led to the development of relevant tools and models, which could subsequently influence how leaders are trained and supported. This enables them to incorporate and consider what may influence and improve their resilience in their leadership role.

As the way of the world is changing and all sectors move towards the triple bottom line approach (Hacking & Guthrie, 2008), the Third Sector could be seen as leading the way in this exploration of resilience. Developing this work and exchanging knowledge across and between sectors is recommended as an approach to take forward. There are examples of good practice and models and tools that could be examined to support this approach. The importance of building cross sector relationships is key to the success of this recommendation and for the programme for government previously discussed in Section 1.1.2.

This study examined a conceptual framework developed from research carried out with "high-flyers" in the corporate world. Although the findings of the research necessitated the development of a reconceptualised model to incorporate the insights from Third-Sector leaders, it is interesting to consider that although there were many differences, there were also many similarities. To go back to the work of Middleton (2016) on cultural intelligence (previously mentioned in Chapter 8), the ability to cross the divides and thrive in multiple cultures is increasingly needed by leaders to succeed in our current times and is thus essential for being a resilient leader in any sector.

Wider Implications

One final thought before completing this section; I noticed that most of the traditional leadership writing on leadership and business doesn't always mention which sector they are based on. There is a presumption that it is the private sector. To go back to our changing times, if we think of the way sport has moved, including women's football, rugby, and cricket teams, the move has been away from calling it "women's football", but still having a way to let us know which team is playing. Could this be an option for leadership books so that we don't always presume it is the "male team" or the private sector?

In today's world, how we view resilience has changed. It is much more something that impacts across all areas of life. The support needed to improve resilience and thus minimise risk of burnout therefore needs to be more holistic. Support frameworks, models, and writing should no longer be separate entities dependent on context, or whether the risk of burnout is at work, due to personal issues, or related to society, sport, or external factors. If the behaviours needed to improve resilience occur across all parts of life, then the support, including the frameworks, the models, and the literature, must be holistic and work through a whole-person approach rather than only on a single part of how a leader lives their life.

The term "fix the roof while sun is shining", which could be thought of as "proactive resilience", is an area to consider. Most leaders interviewed didn't wait until they were at the bottom of the curve before they started to think about resilience behaviours. Instead, they were considered on a daily basis to ensure that the "resilience reservoir" was always topped up and ready to be drawn on. With a current focus on well-being (Kotera et al., 2022), at an individual level, at a global level, and at an economic level, this proactive resilience could be thought of as part of this picture. It sits much more aligned to how we think of wellbeing than the traditional definition of "bouncing back after a setback". Leaders are considering in advance what will make the depth of bounce shallower and the comeback quicker. It could be argued that thinking around wellbeing as a leader, including programmes like active leadership and leadership exchange, are in the early stages of their development, and this work on resilience could be developed in alignment with this theme going forward.

A story quoted in Obama's (2020) book told how his daughters were holding him to account about an oil spill. He used this as an example of how sometimes, as a leader, the weight all sits on your shoulders, and that weight can come from all aspects of life, so it makes sense to think that the answers to being resilient come from all parts of life – and not just work.

I also know from speaking to leaders over the years that the feeling of loneliness in the role can feel even more enhanced when we need to default to "game face" and pretend all of that isn't in our minds. We will, of course, put every ounce of energy into keeping our organisations alive and our beneficiaries supported, but we shouldn't have to pretend we aren't human and that we don't have all these other thoughts racing through our heads at the same time.

It's been a period of huge challenges over recent years. We've seen leaders rising to the occasion and many acts of kindness and support to keep our spirits high. We all worry about our organisations, our staff, and our beneficiaries, but let's not be afraid to be human and acknowledge that we are juggling other concerns too.

Let's continue to share, be there for each other, and not always feel the need to show a brave face, pretend we are confident in what we are doing, and that it won't be a struggle at times. We are all leaders, but we are more than our role, and to ensure our well-being and resilience, we need to recognise this and find support that encompasses a more holistic understanding.

I was recently reminded of the quote:

> When times are good, we always think they will never end and then when times are bad, we always think it will never end, it's human nature, but the facts and history prove every time that they do finish and then we all go again.

It reminded me of another of my favourite quotes (from The Best Exotic Marigold Hotel movie – sorry, not an academic or literary tome!):

> It will be alright in the end. If it's not alright it's not the end.

Final Thoughts

In the latter stages of working on this book, I was invited to visit a friend who had recently moved to another country to start a new phase of life. For her, it wasn't a first time, but for me, as someone who had always lived in the same city (although for the last 20 years, lived between two ends of the country), it seemed like a big step. I saw how she had done her research, taking hard facts alongside her values and what mattered to her and also with how she felt about each geographic area she considered. It felt a privilege to see the journey from when she first mentioned the idea to visit a couple of years later, when it had become a reality.

This was at a time when I was trying to make a big decision about moving permanently to my island home. Having recently lost my stepfather and being worried about my increasingly frail elderly (but still feisty) mother. It felt wrong to be moving further away from her, but I had been thinking about ways I could find of spending longer periods of quality time with her rather than just popping in a couple of times a week. I also felt the pull of a new way of living at this stage of life and a new adventure to be had. I followed my tried and tested way of working. I took a few steps in the direction I wanted to go and, with each step, gauged if it felt I was going in the right direction. I spoke to estate agents to gauge the market for my city home. I sussed out places to stay for my longer visits to my mum. She insisted that I shouldn't make plans based on her – a friend reminded me if it were me, would I want to hold my daughter back, but it didn't stop me feeling selfish/guilty. I got more involved in the highland community, from volunteering, going to classes when I was there, and changing my hairdresser. It was all tiny steps, but that I knew that it would build momentum as my confidence grew, but also that I could change direction if at any time it didn't feel I was heading in the right direction, and in my last days of editing – I find out I'm going to be a grandmother – a whole new adventure unfurls!!

I know my way of doing things can be infuriating for those around me. I explore many paths and have to walk along them to see if they feel right before I can commit to a journey.

So, in this book, I have tried to share what I learnt through my research, what I learnt from my own life as a leader and my more holistic experiences, and what I have had the privilege of learning from the amazing leaders from all sectors who I have worked with during my career.

As I come to the end of writing, I know this book has turned out quite differently to how I planned it (sorry, Routledge!), but it is an example of whole-life resilience. We choose a direction, take small steps, try it out, adapt, build new networks around us for support, try things out and try again if we fail, gather information, keep positive mindsets, and find time to do what keeps us well.

Summary

This chapter has taken us back to the research and summarised the findings and the contributions to both knowledge and practice. It explores what further research may be useful and what lessons have been learnt along the journey, personally, professionally, and holistically. It has also brought together my resilience journey over this final period of writing this book.

Analogy: Each Destination is But a Doorway to Another Journey

I have used this analogy a lot during my lifetime. It's been relevant both when travelling, where I love the unexpected meetings and directions a journey can take – sometimes when you least expect it. But it also links to leading and learning – who thought when entering academia, I would end up writing a book, having a whole new "tribe" of peers, and finding a new world of connections and opportunities?

We always seem to think that once we get to this point, life will be sorted, the stars will align, and we can rest on our laurels/get a bit of a break/have cocktails while watching the sunset, but how often do we really get to this point? Aren't we always looking for the next adventure? Each moment of learning opens our world further shows us more possibilities and opportunities. How can we stop and sit still? Akagi thinking ascertains that we need purpose in life, whether that's doing good, being successful, spending time with family, or whatever is important to you. Don't we always strive for more? This analogy always makes me think that life (and maybe our business strategies) is more a series of stepping stones to help us get to the other side, but once we get there, we may find more previously unseen stepping stones to help us further along the journey.

It reminds me that it's not what you do that will be remembered, but how you make people feel. I hope you have found this book touched you in some way, resonated with how you see resilience for you, and will have some impact, however small, in how you look after yourself and how you see your role as a "holistic" resilient leader.

References

Bonetree, C., Martikke, S., & Wilkinson, S. (2022). *Good Evidence: A Guide to Help Community Organisations Produce Research that Gets Taken Seriously*. Greater Manchester Centre for Voluntary Organisation.

Elkington, J. (1997). *Cannibals with Forks: the Triple Bottom Line of 21st Century Business*. Capstone.

Hacking, T., & Guthrie, P. (2008). A Framework for Clarifying the Meaning of Triple Bottom-Line, Integrated, and Sustainability Assessment. *Environmental Impact Assessment Review*, *28*(2–3), 73–89. https://doi.org/10.1016/J.EIAR.2007.03.002

Kotera, Y., Green, P., & Sheffield, D. (2022). Positive Psychology for Mental Well-being of UK Therapeutic Students: Relationships with Engagement, Motivation, Resilience and Self-Compassion. *International Journal of Mental Health and Addiction*, *20*, 1611–1626. https://doi.org/10.1007/s11469-020-00466-y

Middleton, J. (2016). *Cultural Intelligence*. Bloomsbury Academic.

Obama, B. (2020). *A Promised Land*. Pengiun Random House.

Index

Note: **Bold** page numbers refer to tables and *italic* page numbers refer to figures.